New Media and Development

Edited by

Dr. Dharmendra Singh

Neha Publishers & Distributors

Delhi

Publisher
NEHA PUBLISHERS & DISTRIBUTORS
4832/24,Prahlad Lane,S-207 Ansari
Road, Daryaganj,Delhi-110002
Ph.: 43570976, 23278261

Edition: 2015

ISBN : 978-93-80318-56-1

Laser Typesetting:
JEE-VEE Graphics # 9911902109

Price : ₹ 595.00

Printed: Vikas Computers

Dedicated

to

AKSHAT and ANIRUDH

Preface

Media came into being to connect the two dissimilar poles which are known as sender and receiver who can be from any society, caste, community, gender and can be the follower of any ideology[right or left]. This [connect] was the pure idea which was residing in the mind of the mighty minds of the old made them unrest and compelled them to bring it into sign which can be used as medium. This medium will be very powerful because an ordinary medium cannot connect the century's divided human race like Gandhi's Ahinsa, Raja Ram Mohan Roy's Brahma Samaj, ancient time's Buddha's Nirvna, and so on which were used by these people their means which became messages to others and its impact can be seen in the history of humanity. Marshall McLuhan's Medium is the Message where there is no difference between the two medium and the message sometimes contents become medium and medium become contents or in another word it can be said that medium is content and content is medium which play a very important role to socialise the society, unite and integrate it.It is totally depend on the nature of medium that how much powerful it is because the shape of the society which is connected with powerful bond of values, thoughts and other great ideas can be changed as per demond of time when the medium will be powerful because authority is always challenged by the authority and broken by the authority. Traditional set up of Indian society which was in the vedic period little bit changed in the Upanishdic India and so in the Puranic, Medieval, British and Independent India which is known as modern period and after it Post-Modern set-up of society. Thanks to folk medium to modern whose earlier scope was very much limited and now widening and widening which fulfills the dream of Marshall McLuhan's Global Village which will be done by the modern technology [medium]

The nature and job of the medium is also understood by Habermas who says that the concept of public sphere is changed because of the revolution of new technology where public earlier its meaning was denoted size wise and ideology wise is also changed due to dominated media. Hicky Gazett's [1780]importance Indian known very well, as well as Britishers and similarly other countries too. But, here we should know that the content which was carrying out by it is also important similarly because without it it is meaningless, useless.

Fortunately or unfortunately, the role of modernization, which was expected by D. Lerner, Wilbur Schramm,Eluho Katz,L.Pye and others are infringed by the dominant society, people, state and they used it as an weapon and trading with the developing states. Media traders, who always think about the benefit of their own. Now a days every society's intellectuals are demanding to break the hegemony media. They believe in deconstruction, decolonization, post modernization where they demand that media must not be played by the capitalists' hands and not be institutionalized, centerlized. The very nature of any society is plural and it must be respected. Participation in media as well as content, this plurality must be seen and every religion , community, caste, gender ,region , language, ideology must be included in both media and content, so that everybody can feel 'our media and our content' that is why they must access it and operate it which is not happening

Now, Trinity- politician, capitalist and media people, is ruling the state and behaving like Luise xiv, who was used to say that he is born to rule over the people because he is the State. Now a days all the media institution are run by the capitalists who only and only want benefit/profit rather quality of education. Channels/Print Media houses and other organizations are also run by them. The fee of these courses are so costlier that a common people's sons and daughters cannot study. The benefit of the education can be accessed by the richer of the society which not new thing since centuries it is going on. Interesting thing is here that all the public agencies are helpless, they are not in condition to control the private ventures who are running these private institutions (Education and Media) because they provide funds to run the public agencies. Indirectly, it can be said that all the public agencies and government system are dependent on capitalists (investors). This monopoly is somewhere responsible to break the thin thread of Indian democracy which was earlier also was the motto of Indian media.

The voice of voiceless was expected and it was thought that this job would be done by revolutionary media of the time to remove the country's gap which is like a leprosy in a healthy body became also vein because this task was started by the vested interest people of Indian society who were governed by the colonization principles who never wanted to happen it and establish human society. Karl Popper is his well known book "The Open Society and its Enemies" page no.288 says that 'the Gods are abandoned. But there place is filled by powerful man or group-sinister pressure groups whose wickedness is responsible for all the evils we suffer from- such as Learnel Elders of Zion, the monopolist or the capitalist or the imperialist.' And in a true sense, all the objectives and nouns which are used in above mentioned para by Karl Popper are applied on modern media of our society as well as media institutions where media as a subject is taught which has decided to send the humble and pure hearted people to asylum (Michel Foucault), the place where mad people live.

The owners of modern media are rule over by the conspiracy theory of society who know how to make heaven on earth and that is why they try to counter conspiracy against non-existing conspirators and the same is also done by the media operators/educators. The always try to spread fear in the mind of humble and simple people and compel them to leave the those masters or favour them who directly or indirectly fostering these media houses and those who are governed by the vested interest idealogy.

The new trends, now a days has come in the presentation of the media content where a group of presenters whom God has given all the talent, knowledge to compare and analyses any types of programme which are telecasted by the channels. It seems ridiculous but yes these presenters do all these things shamelessly.

The content of this book is divided into two parts. Part one focuses specifically on new media and its effect on society especially

Indian society where pluralistic population reside and the second part emphasizes on the problem of states/region/gender or may be said about the subaltern/marginalized or Edward Said's Orientalists who want to be out from their present status which is miserable or out of periphery which is known as a fire of help where all their dreams, emotions, aspirations to do something or be something is burnt. Really they are suffering for those faults which are not committed by them. The chapter which are contributed by the contributers are very much meaningful, analytical and have depth inside of the authors regarding the subject which could be understood when it would be read out critically. Some research papers are already presented in the national seminars, but after knowing the importance of them, it is decided that it should be published in a book form and that is why it is tried here, whereas content of these research papers are concerned, these are pure opinion or research of researchers, publisher or editor will have not any responsibility if anything goes wrong.

I am really thankful to all those who directly or indirectly help me to complete this task in my very busy clerical job of headship of the department where academic works comes second. Mr. Chaudhary, my publisher, I am also grateful to you that you once again trusted upon me and decided to publish this work of art. Finally, I owe to my wife and my son who supported me to accomplish this work of art Thanks Contributors.

Date: 3/2/2014

Dr. Dharmendra Singh
Prof. Head of Department
Journalism and Mass Communication (LLIDMS)
Affiliated to GGSIP University
New Delhi-110047

Contents

Convergence: Culture, Language and Identity at Crossroads

Dr. Charu lata Singh*

Convergence: Culture, Language and Identity at Crossroads

Abstract

In wake of the fast emerging new media technologies, public sphere and changing dimensions of culture, language and identity are the issues which are of utmost concern. The public and private spheres of political, economic and social spheres have undergone a visible and prominent change. Though progress and development can not be achieved without moving with the times and adopting the latest technologies, the basic values need not compromised with. New technologies have enabled the individuals to interact on different platforms at the same time. They have given rise to a new intercultural persona in individuals across the globe. There is a shift from individualization to universalisation; from one to one and from one to all; from recipient to provider, where technology is the root cause for assimilation and homogenization of cultures and where the new forms of interactions, socialization and expression are the order of the day, the new media technologies have democratized and globalized the information and have lead to a cultural shift from 'sit back and told' culture to a 'making and doing culture' and exchanging it with

* Professor, HOD
Vivekananda School of Journalism and Mass Communication, VIPS
(Affiliated to Guru Gobind Singh Indraprastha University, Delhi)

others. In these processes of moving fast, somewhere the basic human touch and human values are getting back seat or are getting lost. Though whole new environment has been created for questioning and exploring atmosphere which have facilitated new ideas, thoughts and creative expressions to be exhibited, however on the other side,the quality is being replaced by quantity. The social networking sites are creeping and eroding deep into our relationships, our cultures and ourselves. These fast changing dimensions certainly need self-regulation or self constrain in relation to culture, language and identities which at the crossroads today.

Keywords: Role of convergence, changing environments, eroding culture, language and identities, diluting and changing values.

Introduction

Culture, language and identity are the issues of concern for the social, political and communication thinkers today. Culture emanates from interpretative procedures, discourses, myths, stories and array of artifacts that constructs the concepts and ideology of a society. Socio-cultural, socio-economic and political environments play a decisive role in shaping of the culture, language and identities in a society at a any given time. Language and cultural contexts can be identified as- the values of elite and masses, the societal values, the media structures, ethics etc. Culture is defined by Carey as a 'process' which itself is a reflection of the complexity of the phenomenon. It can be argued though, that " the fantasies and 'ideas' of 'the world' have been there since Plato described in his Timaeus the history of the world; since Aristotle defined the 'world state'; since Francis Bacon distinguished between different world concepts 'global terrestris' and 'globus intellectualis'. In the process of cultural change, innovation has played a significant role, as the process of evolution is continuous. The fusion of newer concepts and ideas regenerate different forms of creative expressions to do away with the older and prevalent ones, which subsequently get degenerated or mutilated. It is like a tree which unfolds in every season to erupt, to grow, to deliver, and in doing so it withstands the adverse conditions. The innovation results in evolution. The degree of evolution depends on the capacity of exchange of information and acceptance by the society and its sense of cultural identity and self-usage. The whole process though needs control mechanisms at various levels so that the positive creative expressions result through the phases of transition rather than resulting in erosion and dilution.

Era of Erosion and Dilution

It is very modest to say that we are living in times of globalised culture, homogenous culture or to say that we are passing through the times of transition. The phases of transition are to evolve from lower to higher levels but if they evolve too fast without taking cultural abd environmental considerations into account they stand to wither fast. What we witness today is not the phase of transition, especially when we talk in terms of culture, language and identity as we see total degradation. It may sound pessimistic point of view, but the way the culture, language and Identity are getting eroded make evident and forces to believe that we are living in times of dilution and erosion and not in times of transitions because the change is abrupt and for worse in culture language and identity. It is clearly evident and is visible if we observe and analyze today's day to day incidents of killings, rapes, accidents, agitations, corruption etc. the list may go unexhausted, which reflect on the emerging culture, language and identity. There is erosion of values and traditions ; national, regional and even English language; identity today has no meaning in the sense as it was considered earlier.

In the fast changing society the fabric of culture, language and Identity has got loosened. The erosion and dilution can be seen and derived right through the basic unit of the society i.e. from the family to society to state. Needless to say that the erosion or dilution in all the units narrows down to the individual, his behaviour, his integrity, his conduct and his personality. What is disturbing today is the very fact of dilution and erosion of civilized attitudes, values, behavior, mannerisms and languages.

Culture: Culture is an amalgamation of language, religion, customs, traditions,behaviors and values. Each culture tells to have a wider plane of understanding. Cultures need to be preserved. They need to be allowed to evolve but should not be allowed to let go, to perish.

Language: The indigenous languages, their originality and purity are heading towards extinction. World data shows 80 major languages such as Mandarin and Russian are spoken by 80 percent other 3500 small languages are being preserved by 0.2 percent in the world.

Identities Reasons for loss of identities is the individualized culture, unitary /nuclear families, hectic life styles, active commercial and market trends, where every thing is a commodity which can be bought and sold. The values and emotions are taking a back seat. If we start analyzing with the basic institution of society, which is considered to be sacred, has got diluted. The children born in unit families depend on the maids and servants and pick up a lot from them which adds in forming their personalities and individualities: their culture, language and identity emanates from these very factors. .The generations are being brought up by the maids and servants and nannies and not by grand parents, parents or gurus or acharyas. The environmental factors given to an individual right from the beginning in order to grow have lasting impacts.

In a wider spectrum, the cultural diversity is leading to changes in indigenous cultural values and ethos and in deeper sense in dilution and to erosion.

Theoretical Viewpoints

Identity has always been fluid and a subject of change under social, political and economic pressures. The change in the identity can be positive or negative. There are whole range of difficulties and challenges that may arise against the dominant cultures and identities. The identities formed in the cultural experiences which are in contest, give rise to 'identity crises'. The sense of ourselves can be affected by the process injected with global socio-political and cultural change. The complexity of such changes assume new and different identities laden with supremacy and signification. Also, where the systematic distortion of the culture takes place as a consequence of growth of technology and access to it, it does give rise to moral panics and conflicts between conservatives and modernists.

Rabindra Nath Tagore aptly remarked, "All traditional structures of art must have sufficient degree of elasticity to allow it to respond to varied impulses of life, delicate or virile, to grow with its growth, to dance with its rhythm."

Poster (1995), argues that rational argument, reminiscent of a public sphere, can rarely prevail and consensus achievement is not possible online, specifically because identity is defined very differently online.

To quote Marshall McLuhan, "Time" has ceased, "space" has vanished. We now live in a global village.... a simultaneous happening.'

In relation to the statement above the Alvin Toffler expressed, "We live in a Cairo bazaar of competing models. In this psychological phantasmagoria we search for a new style, a new way of ordering our existence". In the classic book Future Shock, he observed that advanced industrial technology was accelerating the velocity of cultural change, thus creating a chaotic "Cairo bazaar" in which many cultural styles compete and coexist as models for human living. In this vision, production and media technologies have created and made us aware of many different possible lifestyles from around the world, each of which simultaneously exists in a chaotic cultural landscape.

Changing Values: Trust Deficit Society

Values are changing at all levels. Be in at individual level or state level. Dilution and erosion is taking place at all levels from all sides.

Individual and Family System: The very institution of family is at crossroads today. There is visible dilution of the authority of elders in the family. Not to adhere to certain practices is considered a fashion. There is visible change in the value system. Erosion of commitments to the family, its values and traditions. There is erosion of relationships; whether husband wife; brother-sister; parents and children or friends. Recent suicides and killing are the evident examples.

Society: Erosion of cordial relations in the neighborhood. Un concerned behaviours of people with impulsive characters is the concern. Social values and norms along with basic curtsies seen to be missing. Care for social values, for heritage, our for past is getting lost. There is dilution of social setup and erosion of social fabric.

Political values: High level rampant corruption ; erosion of political commitments; loss of interest of people in mechanisms of politics.; Political institutions, political offices right from the lower to the office of president or of military or prime minister which are the sacred offices for the functioning democracy; voting patterns; Visible behaviours in parliaments and legislatures; erosion of true democratic values; dilution in participatory culture are matters of deliberation.

Economic values: There seems to be complete erosion of value of money and value for money. Dilution of money power as money power is put to use for menial purposes; involvement of the highest offices in corruption; market forces paramount and individual welfare at the back seat are shameful developments.

The developments which try to take turns to justify the wrong behaviors, actions or doers are the matters of concern. When the change starts taking the shape of dilution and then erosion and subsequently, when this erosion goes to the extent of crossing the limits resulting in shamelessness without any remorse are definitely matters of deliberation for all thinking beings.

Change/transformation→Dilution→Erosion→Shamelessness

To put the positive point of view, one may claim that we are opening up or coming out of the garb of conservative ethos and ideals we are adopting the cultures of the outside world, but the fact is that, no culture teaches to behave, act and react in the manners which is evident through the day to day events.. Every culture enshrines good values. No culture would teach to disrespect, disgrace, indulge in corrupt, violent, pornographic and malicious practices at public places or at the places of public concern. In a nutshell, basic human thinking and reasoning and controlling of self conscious and self regulated behaviours and values are getting eroded. The whole culture is affected.

Loss of culture→Loss of language→Lost identity→Loss of trust

Language dies when culture is diluted, it erodes identity. Due to which self confidence is lost, this adds to erosion of happiness and peace and leads to depression and other malaiscs, resulting in abrupt and instant impulsive behaviors and reactions resulting in and producing results contrary to the cultural values and traditions . There is dilution in individual behavior in truthfulness or honesty. What we see today are the eroded individualistic identities, characters have got diluted to loose their own identities and personalities. The result is trust deficit society.

To quote Alvin Toffler, "Society needs people who take care of elderly and who know how to be compassionate and honest, society needs people who work in hospitals, society needs all kinds of skills that are not just cognition; they are emotional they are affectionate, you cannot run the society on data and computers alone." Toffler cites, ' Herbert Gerjuoy', "Tomorrows illiterate will not be the man who can't read ; he will be the man who has not learned how to learn."

Convergence

New media technologies have allowed people to increase accessibility to a broad range of media and globalization has even allowed media audiences themselves to gain access to more various entertainment programmes through T.V. and cinema. Internet has become the Media with wide access and interactivity. It has allowed various culture, languages and identities to ameliorate to give rise to their diluted versions. Internet has provided fluidity to various concepts values and traditions among various sub cultures which adopt quickly to change to give rise to loosely affiliated concepts and norms. Media also plays an effective role in making and breaking of culture, language and identities. Also, in the processes of Mass production and mass consumption, where Producer + consumer+ Prosumers are becoming one and where we are moving from hierarchy to weirdarchy ; from reality we are moving towards virtuality but now the virtuality has started traveling to real world....that is the phenomenon each one of us need to be worried about. Cultural identities are changing at the ever faster rate due to new media's ever changing and penetrating technologies. The big challenge in front of new media is to suppress the negative and promote the positive aspects of the cultures so that it can give rise to cultural identities laden with all positive and pervasive values. The media thus, should make all the possible efforts to promote positivity and suppress negativity.

Future Implications

Unless the strong parameters are adopted for keeping values, the whole process of continuity of culture may become chaotic. The culture which is not confined to any kind of physical barriers may create confusions. The ongoing process of comprehensive growth and evolution entails the questions of sufficient conditions for cultural resistance or submission. It clearly suggests that only the dominant values will survive (positive or negative), will give rise to the culture which will be extremely positive or extremely negative. Thus extreme polarization would take place. Hence, the end result of the whole process will be the homogenised culture either, with all the positive ingredients or with all the negative ingredients. There will be survival of the fittest.

The question we face at the dawn of network culture is whether we, the inhabitants of our networked publics, can reach across our micro-clustered worlds to coalesce into a force capable of understanding the condition we are in. Can we produce positive change without disturbing the indigenous fabrics of the societies. It important to give time to grasp, analyse and adopt, as the erosion and dilution is engulfing the deep rooted cultural values at an unimaginable pace. The multiple layers of sheets of Indian cultural values is being pierced form all sides and corners. The culture, language and identities standing at the crossroads, need helping hand of each one in the society

References:

1. Albrow M. and King E. (1990) .'Globalisation, Knowledge and Society'. London: Sage Publications.
2. Alvin Toffler, interview by Norman Swann, Australia Broadcast Corporation Radio National, "Like matters", 5th March, 1998)
3. Alvin Toffler, Future shock (1970) New York: Random House
4. Castells, Manuel (1996) The Rise of the Network Society. Oxford: Blackwell.

Comment by Sarvesh Dutt Tripathi

The paper has been written by Dr. Charu who is senior to me in teaching hierarchy therefore it will not be adequate to make any comment, yet I have some humble views of myself :

It appears to be a view of the researcher rather research paper. All the facts presented are apparent in the surrounding and accurate but the writer has not established how new media or convergence is mainly responsible for socio political, economic, cultural, or whatsoever it is, erosion being observed in the society. The objective, in my opinion, of the paper should be more transparent and exhaustive so that the reader may correlate it with the inference. (With due apology)

Participatory monitoring of Communication for social change for Gender Based Violence (GBV) prevention

Dr. Manisha Rathor*

Overview

Participation is not simply a fringe benefit that authorities may grant as a concession, but a human being's birthright that no authority can deny... What is a participative society? I must confess that it is easier for me to explain what a non-participative one is. All I have to do is point to our present society, one in which social classes live in separate worlds, in a rigid order of domination, oppression and exploitation. Let us briefly discuss communication approaches used in development and, in particular, the distinctive features of Communication for Social Change (CFSC). We go on to consider CFSC and its importance for Gender based violence (GBV) prevention and care.

Communication and Participation

When communication process are used to inform people enable them to contribute their points of view, reach consensus and carry

* Associate Professor,
MBCEM,
(Affiliated to Guru Gobind Singh Indraprastha University, Delhi)

out an agreed change or development action together, it can be said that communication is participation. Two main types of communication approaches for development.

1. Communication approaches based on modernization theories and information persuasion strategies used by industries. Examples include Diffusion of Innovations, social marketing, Information-Education-Communication (IEC), Behavior Change Communication (BCC)
2. Communication approaches based on critical theory, collective learning, and information sharing and dialogic processes forged during social and political struggles against colonial and dictatorial powers imposed on poor communities and countries. Examples include Participatory communication for social change.

Distinction between the 2 sets of approaches is not so clear in practice. For example both can be more or less "participatory" depending on the facilitation skills of the change agents involved and the timelines of sponsoring agencies- government or non-government. Over recent years, there have also been important areas of convergence between the two sets of approaches. For example, there is now a fairly universal agreement that communication should focus on change at both individual and societal levels, and that "tangible" (e.g., service uptake) as well as "intangible" (e.g., community empowerment) outcomes need to be measured.

Communication for Social Change (CFSC)

Whenever participatory communication approaches are adopted, communication: changes its role from that of a vehicle for information-persuasion to that of a tool for dialogue and inter-service coordination - which is absolutely essential for participation in problem identification, problem articulation and problem solving. CFSC in some ways has always been around. It was only in 1997, however, when the Rockefeller Foundation organized a series of meetings to discuss the role of "Communication in Social Change" that the characteristics and theoretical underpinnings of CFSC began to emerge. CFSC can be defined as a process of public and private dialogue through which people themselves define who they are, what they need and how to get what they need in order to improve their own lives. It utilizes dialogue that leads to collective problem identification, decision-making and community-based implementation of solutions to development issues. Social Change can be defined as: a positive change in peoples' lives - as they themselves define such change. CFSC questions an approach to development that: does not include the population that is directly affected. CFSC promotes a communication process that supports effective community participation, particularly of the most impoverished and marginalized sectors of society.

CFSC practitioners use a "bottom-up" approach by placing ownership, access and control of communication directly in the hands of affected communities. This shifts control of media, messages, tools and content of communication from the powerful to the traditionally powerless.

Ultimately, using such skills, previously powerless communities can become "self-renewing" - able to manage their own communication processes for their own good. Similar to other participatory communication approaches, the process of CFSC is a "product" in and of itself. The process helps individuals and communities build a stronger capacity to communicate in person, through the arts or using media and other communication technologies. CFSC does not attempt to anticipate which media, messages or techniques are better. The participation of social actors, who are in turn communicators, takes place within a process of collective growth that precedes the creation of messages and products such as a radio program, a video documentary or a pamphlet. Messages and their dissemination are just additional elements of the communication process. CFSC's focus is on the dialogue process through which people are able to identify obstacles and develop communication structures, policies, processes and media or other communication tools to help them achieve the goals they themselves have outlined and defined. Rather than focusing on persuasion and information dissemination, CFSC promotes dialogue, debate and negotiation from within communities. Rather than confining dialogue to an airing of grievances or a discussion of information, CFSC supports focused deliberation, collective decision-making and collective action.

Communication for Social Change (CFSC) and Gender based violence (GBV)

In India, gender-based violence perpetrated against women is an extremely complex issue resulting from and perpetuated by various societal, economic and cultural factors. Gender-based violence has been increasingly recognized around the world as a grave challenge for public health and development and as a violation of human rights. As women's groups have galvanized attention and momentum for action, a wide range of initiatives across the Nation have directed their efforts towards mitigating, preventing and responding to such violence, while significant progress has been made in recognizing gender-based violence as a serious public health problem and a grave human rights concern, the continued prevalence of such violence reveals that not enough progress has been made. The need for collaborative, holistic efforts that engage the community in challenging the discriminatory norms and stigmatizing attitudes that perpetuate violence and in responding meaningfully to survivors' immediate and long-term needs. Gender-based violence is physical, mental or social violence and abuse (including sexual violence) that includes acts (attempted or threatened) carried out with or without force and without the consent of the victim. The violence is directed against a person because of her or his gender (because she is a woman or because he is a man) or gender role in a society or culture. Forms of gender violence include sexual violence, sexual abuse, sexual harassment, sexual exploitation, early or forced marriage, discrimination, the denial of food, education or freedom, domestic violence and incest. In 1993, the United Nations General Assembly adopted the Declaration on the Elimination of Violence against Women, defining violence against women as "any act of gender-based violence that results in, or is likely to result in, physical, sexual or psychological harm or suffering to women, including threats of such acts, coercion or arbitrary deprivation of liberty, whether occurring in public or in private life." Why does this violence continue? The Declaration on the Elimination of Violence against Women, highlights violence against women as "a manifestation of historically unequal power relations between men and women, which have led to domination over and discrimination against women by men and to the prevention of the full advancement of women." Prevailing gender norms and attitudes about the acceptability of violence continue to fuel gender-based violence in the region, as in the rest of the world. By working proactively to energize momentum against violence, initiatives for preventing GBV also empower women living with violence to speak out and seek assistance.

Gender refers to the socially determined differences between men and women. These differences encompass roles, responsibilities, opportunities, privileges, expectations, and limitations prescribed to males and to females in any culture: they are socially constructed, context based, and learned through socialization, and they determine many aspects of relationships between males and females as well as among females and among males. Although gendered roles and responsibilities can change over time within and across cultures, they are often deeply rooted in long-standing assumptions societies hold about women, men, boys, and girls. In virtually every society around the world, these assumptions tend to reinforce patriarchal norms and values, or systems by which males hold more power than females in both private and public domains and, to differing degrees, exercise this greater power as a basic entitlement. To the extent that gender roles are used to both preserve and maintain women's subordinate status in relation to men, gender has been identified as one of the most important underlying factors promoting violence against women: in fact, violence against women is often referred to as? gender-based violence.

But while mass education campaigns aimed at changing individual behavior play an essential role in GBV prevention and care, without deep-rooted social change they are highly unlikely to be sustainable. Social, cultural and political factors underpin the so-called "risk behaviors." These factors include, but are not limited to: poverty, inequality, prejudice, the status of women, the responsibility of men, marginalization and disempowerment, gender based violence, community and social cohesion, and many others. Sustaining a change in behaviors or social conditions is fundamentally about fostering and supporting communication in society.

Evaluating Communication for Social Change

But how do we know Communication for Social Change is working? This is a central question. It immediately makes us think about "indicators." Indeed, the question of "what indicators?" tends to grab our attention, whereas the equally important question of "who should develop and use these indicators?" is often overlooked. In addition to focusing on process and outcome measures, following principles for CFSC measurement can be used:

- CFSC measurement tools must be community-based and participatory.
- The tools/methods must be SUM: Simple, Understandable and Measurable.
- The tools/methods must be developed with input from people from developing countries.

- o Assessment of CFSC impact should look at impact on the short-term, intermediary and long-term.

One CFSC evaluation challenge is to determine how best to measure short-term increases in community communication capacity, and in turn, how to measure the contribution this increasing capacity is making to broad, longer-term social change and more narrowly defined improvements, for example, in GBV prevention and care. It is assumed that the CFSC process will work most effectively if the "community" can build-and build on-its capacity for communication at the individual and collective levels. The more capacity for individuals and groups, the more voice can be expressed and heard. The more the dialogue ... The more the stage for collective action. The more a story of success ... the more a community can solve the next problem and continually renew itself. Some of the information that dialogue members might consider as evidence of communication capacity might include strong communication skills and a high degree of "connectedness" (horizontal and vertical).

Literature Review

This paper is largely but not exclusively confined to the English language. Bibliographical databases for the health and social sciences were searched with a mix of thesauri terms for evaluation and research methodologies combined with key words and key phrases including participatory evaluation, participatory research, and participatory monitoring. The truncated term participate was also used with a range of methodological thesauri terms as were keyword combinations of participatory with evaluate, measure, assesse or monitore. Communication Abstracts, Sociological Abstracts and Worldwide Political Science Abstracts. Supplementary database searches were undertaken on author names where a depth of knowledge in the field by an individual was identified from the literature. Where research monographs and conference proceedings were identified these were located through library catalogue searches and retrieved. Two Internet search engines, Google and Alltheweb were also used. Key word and key phrase combinations (as explained above) were used to identify major agencies involved with the use of PM&E methodologies. Agencies with a substantial Internet presence in this field included: the World Bank; the United Nations Development Program; the Food and Agriculture Organization (FAO) of thc United Nations.

International and the Participatory Development Forum. The websites of these agencies were examined to identify relevant documents and in some cases bibliographies compiled by experts in the field. The major reports and papers are referenced in this document.

Participatory Monitoring and Evaluation. What is it?

Participatory Monitoring and Evaluation is by no means new. It draws upon more than 20 years of participatory research traditions such as participatory action research (PAR), participatory rural appraisal (PRA), and farming systems research (FSR).40 During the 1970s, PM&E entered the policy-making domain of large donor agencies and development organizations such as the Food and Agriculture Organization (FAO), United States Agency for International Development (USAID), the Danish International Development Agency (DANIDA), the UK Department for International Development (DFID), and the World Bank. The beginnings of PM&E can also be traced to the growing appreciation for individual and organizational learning among the private sector. And even though interest in PM&E processes has been growing, it should be noted that many local forms of PM&E still go unnoticed. Communities and Community-Based Organizations (CBOs) have long been monitoring and evaluating their work (without using the label of PM&E).

According to Brisolara, two main streams of PM&E have emerged from quite different historical and ideological roots:

1. **Practical PM&E -** focusing on the pragmatic with a central function of fostering evaluation use. Practical PM&E arose in the 1980s primarily in the US and Canada. Geared toward program, policy or organizational decision making, Practical PM&E improves planned-change within programs. Within Practical PM&E efforts, evaluation impact is extended to include organizational learning and change. Practical PM&E is similar to "developmental evaluation" (Patton 1997) and "stakeholder-based evaluation" (Mark and Shotland 1985), but the latter is less concerned with implementation-stage process decisions (monitoring) and more with final, end-of-program, summative evaluation questions.

2. **Transformative PM&E -** based on emancipation and social-justice activism and focuses on empowerment of oppressed groups. Transformative PM&E arose in the 1970s, notably in Latin America, India and Africa - in part as a reaction to scientific models of inquiry that were considered exploitive and detached from urgent social and economic problems.Transformative PM&E efforts aim to democratize social change and as such are similar to "empowerment evaluation" (Fetterman 2001) and "democratic evaluation" (McTaggart 1991).

   Transformative PM&E is underpinned by three key concepts:

   - Who creates and controls the production of knowledge? Transformative PM&E aims to empower people through participation in the process of constructing and respecting their own knowledge (based on Freire's notion of "conscientization") and through their understanding of the connections among knowledge, power and control. Popular knowledge is assumed to be as valid and useful as scientific knowledge.
   - How is the evaluation conducted? The distance between the evaluator and the evaluated is broken down; all participants are contributors working collectively. Initiating and sustaining

genuine dialogue among actors leads to a deep level of understanding and mutual respect.

o Critical reflection. Requires participants to question, to doubt, and to consider a broad range of social factors, including their own biases and assumptions. Although these two streams of PM&E are distinguishable from one another on the basis of their central goals, functions, and historical and ideological roots, there is clearly an overlap between the two.

What is Participatory Monitoring & Evaluation (PM&E)?

So what exactly is PM&E? There is no single definition or methodology for PM&E due to the diverse range of field experiences and the difficulty in reaching agreement on terms such as "monitoring," "evaluation," "community" and "participation." As noted above, PM&E is best described as: a set of principles and a process of engagement in the monitoring and evaluation endeavour. The process is at least as important as the recommendations and results contained in PM&E reports or feedback meetings. Much literature on PM&E has emerged from the international and community-development fields. Perhaps what is unique about PM&E is its emphasis on the inclusion of a wider sphere of stakeholders in the M&E process than more conventional approaches. PM&E practitioners believe that stakeholders who are involved in development planning and implementation should also be involved in monitoring changes and determining indicators for "success." PM&E's fundamental values are trust, ownership and empowerment.

Why use PM&E?

It is important to regard people as agents rather than objects; agents who are capable of analyzing their own situations and designing their own solutions. Conventional M&E is often based on quantitative, non-participatory surveys designed by evaluators external to the program or project in question. These processes have been increasingly criticized for being "top-down," serving only the interests of funding agencies and policy makers, and providing little if any opportunities for all stakeholders to voice their opinions and judgments. Information is typically extracted from populations/ communities/families/participants and concentrated at the top of organizations (usually far removed from beneficiaries), where it often remains underutilized. Conventional M&E has been viewed largely as a form of "policing."The idea of stakeholder participation in evaluation is now widely accepted within the evaluation community. According to Estrella et al (2000), interest in PM&E has grown as a result of several factors, including:

- The growing demand for greater accountability and demonstrable impact.
- The move towards devolution of central government responsibilities and authority to lower levels of government, necessitating new forms of oversight to ensure transparency and to improve support to constituency responsive initiatives.
- Stronger capacities and experiences of Non-Government Organizations (NGOs) and Community-Based Organizations (CBOs) as decision makers and implementers in the development process.
- Mounting evidence that participatory approaches for issue identification and resolution, program design, monitoring and evaluation produce positive results.

Making a PM& E plan for GBV prevention

a) Orient stakeholders to PM&E and set the agenda

Stakeholders can be oriented to a PM&E process during initial planning workshops. Terms of reference for the core PM&E team can be drawn up by stakeholders during these workshops.

Other questions to ask at this point include: Who else should participate? How many participants? How will they participate and at what juncture? How much participation? Depth of participation can range from "shallow" consultation (with no decision-making control or responsibility) to "deep" participation (full involvement in all aspects of an evaluation from design, data collection, analysis and reporting to decisions about dissemination of results and use).

b) Clarify the question: who wants to know what and why?

1. What difference is the communication strategy making? Does it influence dialogue processes between individuals and between groups in terms of tolerance, respect, social justice and active participation? If so, how? If not, why not?
2. Is the communication strategy strengthening individual and community communication capacity, decision making and action? If so, how? If not, why not?
3. Have obstacles to social change been identified? What is being done about them?
4. Are CFSC structures, policies, processes and communication tools being developed? What would facilitate their development?
5. Does the communication strategy enable previously powerless individuals and communities to take control of the means and content of communication, to achieve their own social change goals? If so, how?

Posing such questions helps in the development of PM&E objectives - statements of intent that begin with the words such as: "To assess..." or "To measure..." or "To monitor..." or "To evaluate..." Ideally, PM&E objectives should be derived from the goals of the CFSC initiative or program - for example, what the CFSC teams are aiming to achieve in relation to GBV prevention and care.

c) Identify indicators that will provide the information needed

Follow-up workshops with all stakeholders provide ideal opportunities to present draft PM&Eobjectives. Bringing stakeholders together again to identify what information is needed andwhich information is critical helps to reconfirm the program goals and views on change,information needs, and people's values. Once stakeholders agree on the PM&E objectives, indicators will need to be identified. The procedures for indicator development are not always clear or straightforward, especially when different stakeholders with different priorities and needs are involved. Selecting indicators is therefore: one of the most difficult steps in setting up a PM&E approach, even if those involved accept that good-rather than perfect-indicators are adequate... [This step] highlights, more than any other, the different information needs and expectations that the different stakeholders have of the monitoring work. GBV communication teams should take particular note of the following:

- Additional flexibility in identifying indicators is required when dealing with projects or programs that are themselves participatory in nature - such as the proposed CFSC applications to HIV/AIDS. These types of projects: commonly start tentatively with small interventions based on participatory appraisals or with capacity building activities. Only after discussions have created consensus about development activities will more substantial and focused activities be formulated. During the course of such projects, new partners often join, new insights are generated and new development goals emerge. With the change comes the need to review existing indicators.
- The more groups involved in the PM&E process, the more likely the need to shift from pre-defined and 'objective' indicators to 'negotiated' and context-specific indicators. Knowing how to facilitate the negotiation of indicators amongst stakeholders therefore becomes critical, as different views and priorities need to be reduced to a limited number of indicators. Such negotiations can reinforce a shared vision

of social change particularly when working with groups that differ strongly. Decision makers at every level and scale: from an individual within the household to national and international policy makers will find very different kinds of indicators relevant to their decisions.

- o In many cases, different stakeholder groups usually agree on a set of common indicators, while in other cases multiple sets of indicators may need to be identified to address the different information needs of different stakeholder groups. Indicators need not be perfect - only sufficiently relevant and accurate for those who are going to interpret the information to be able to do so. While there are no set rules to select indicators, one guideline is to use the acronym SMART: indicators should be Specific, Measurable, Action- oriented, Relevant, and Time-bound. The following questions are also helpful to ask when selecting indicators:
- o Is the focus of the PM&E objective a parameter that can be measured accurately and reliably?
- o Are there alternative measures that need to be considered?
- o What resources (human and financial) does the indicator require?
- o Are there any additional measures that would help in interpreting the results of the PM&E objective?

Checklist for questions to be raised while conducting PM&E for GBV

- " Are meeting times and spaces creating opportunities for all the participants people to speak, be heard and contribute to making decisions?
- " How and where does private and public dialogue take place? In relation to the issues of concern, what increase or other changes have there been in:
    - o Family discussion?
    - o Discussion among friends?

- o Discussion in community gatherings?
- o Problem-solving dialogue?
- o New ways of sharing relevant information?
- o Coverage and discussion in news media?
- o Focus and discussion in entertainment media?
- o Debate and dialogue in the political process?

" Are more people from all community groups involved in dialogue about the issues?

" To what extent do participants listen, evaluate information before they use it, challenge rumor and articulate their voice in private and public?

" Have there been improvements in these areas?

" Who is creating and telling the stories around the issues? Is that changing?

" What are the cultural norms those stories reveal? Are they changing?

" Has the community created more opportunities members to discuss issues other than GBV?

" Are new connections between different groups being established within the community, either through face-to-face encounters or using technology?

" Are members of the community making their views known to those who hold official power? How? Is this changing?

" Are community members connecting with outside allies, communities and groups who support of their efforts?

Source: Hunt, J. (2004) Notes on Communication for Social Change, in process.

Synthesizing, analyzing and verifying the data

Analysis of data will also include data validation among stakeholders. Data should be presented back to participants for verification and collective analysis. Ways to ensure feedback and validation occurs include workshops and meetings, distribution of reports (with follow-up interviews), transcripts of interviews returned to interviewees.

How is the data being used and for whose benefit?

This step serves as an important means of disseminating findings and learning from others' experiences. This can be a major problem in some countries. Core team members should seek agreement with stakeholders (through meetings) on how the findings are to be used and by whom. Several versions of PM&E reports may be required, each tailored to different requirements and capacities of different stakeholders. Possible areas of future work should be discussed for follow-up. At this key moment, core PM&E teams should also clarify with stakeholders if the PM&E process needs to be sustained, and if so, how. The PM&E process may need to be adjusted accordingly.

Dimension of Work	**Indicators of Progress**	**Indicators of change and longer term impact**
1.Policy change e.g. Legislative change	• Increased dialog on an issue • Raised profile of issue • Changed Opinion • Changed rhetoric and written publication	• Changed Policy • Change in Legislation Policy/Legislation change implemented • • Positive change in peoples lives as a result of the policy/legislation change
2.Strengthening Civil Society by working with NGO"s Movements/networks Community based organization	• Change in individual members skills, capacity, knowledge and effectiveness • Greater synergy of aims/activities in networks / movements	Civil groups active in influencing decision makers in ways that will benefit the cause.
3.Enlarging democratic space or the space in which civil society groups can effectively operate in society	Greater freedom of expression Increased legitimacy of civil society groups	Change in accountability and transparency of public institutions
4.Supporting people centered policy making	Greater awareness of individual rights and the power systems that withhold rights	Improved access to basic rights such as health, housing water and food.

Conclusions and Challenges

This study was done to find the solution for ever growing problem of Gender based Violence. How media and communication can be used effectively to change the perception of people mostly male member of the society so that this type of violence can be prevented. It is intended to support communication strategies following CFSC principles in GBV prevention and care programs. A new set of M&E principles for CFSC (the "Nairobi principles") were developed during a communication planning meeting at the end of 2003 attended by representatives from a range of national programs and organizations, together with staff from UNICEF and other international organizations. These critiques and principles formed the backdrop to this study - the process, indicators, and tools used to identify, collect and analyze information to measure CFSC must be: simple; community-based; participatory; relatively inexpensive; and context-specific.

A broad range of literature in order to highlight the rationale for using a participatory approach to monitoring and evaluating Communication for Social Change was done. The literature reinforces the notion that CFSC practitioners should facilitate the development of M&E questions, indicators and tools with stakeholders rather than apply pre-determined objectives, measures and methods on stakeholders. Our aim in writing this report, therefore, is to help guide GBV communication teams as they themselves negotiate with stakeholders how CFSC should be monitored and evaluated, and thereby develop new or improved models of M&E most appropriate for their work. The initial CFSC evaluation challenge is to determine how best to measure short-term increases in community communication capacity, and in turn, how to attribute this increasing capacity to broad, longer-term social change and more narrowly defined improvements in GBV prevention and care. But there are other challenges that the teams will need to address.

a) Maintaining flexibility while ensuring information can be generalized How best can micro-level data generated from flexible PM&E be generalized and used to inform national and macro-level strategies and policies? This question is extremely challenging and one that has yet to be answered by PM&E studies.

b) Institutionalizing PM&E Knowledge, Attitudes, Behaviors, and Practices (KABP) surveys, "extractive" forms of social research such as rapid assessment procedures, and Behavioral Surveillance Surveys are still very much the "norm." Improving data quality and building local M&E capacity also preoccupy the managers of existing M&E systems in many HIV/AIDS and other development programs.

The rationale and methodology of Participatory Monitoring and Evaluation. One of the major challenges will be determining how to add or integrate PM&E approaches into conventional M&E systems already challenged by data quality and resource constraints. At what pace and on what scale should PM&E be institutionalized into GBV programs? Can PM&E be built into the standard operating procedures of formal institutions? What type of capacity building in PM&E is needed, for whom, and at what level (personal/individual, organizational/institutional, etc.? How will PM&E capacity be maintained in GBV programs?

Key observations and recommendations

- There is need for more participatory communication initiatives in crisis affected settings, especially to address GBV, HTP, and related issues. There is currently a dearth of such programs, which have the benefit of engaging community members in processes of reflection and dialogue around positive change.
- It is important to carry out culturally-sensitive formative work at the community level, particularly among women and girls, to help ensure that issues such as GBV and the effects of conflict on women's welfare are addressed in appropriate ways.

- o There is a need for more community-driven participatory communication initiatives tailored to local contexts and priorities. Organizations should actively engage community members in discussions to identify concerns and possible solutions, as well as materials and modes of outreach that will be most appropriate and effective. Higher levels of participation strengthen positive outcomes.
- o A deliberate focus on capacity-building and acquisition of new skills (interpersonal, technical, etc.) among community members, and the provision of new opportunities for women and girls, should be integral aspects of participatory communication initiatives, especially those addressing GBV, HTP, and related issues.
- o Participatory communication initiatives should include the strengthening and mobilization of existing peer groups and networks as resources for positive change.
  - " Implementing agencies and local partners and donors should develop methods for improved dissemination and sharing of communication program experiences to enable greater cross-learning and wider adaptation of effective approaches.
  - " Inclusion of various sectors of society, including men and boys in program activities and to track participation through appropriate monitoring systems

References

http://unfpa.ru/assets/files/bcc-manual-eng.pdf

http://www.mrap.info/docs/participatory_ communication_for_social_change.pdf

http://www.unesco.kz/publications/ci/hq/Approaches%20Development%20Communication/CHP8.PDF

http://www.unfpa.org/upload/lib_pub_file/531_filename_combating_gbv_en.pdf

" Uphoff, N. (1989) A field methodology for participatory self-evaluation PPP group and inter-group association performance. Food and Agriculture Organization of the United Nations (FAO); USAID (1996) Performance monitoring and evaluation tips. Conducting a participatory evaluation. Washington D.C: USAID, Center for Development Information and Evaluation, No 1;

" Estrella, M. (2000) 'Learning from Change.' In Estrella, M. with Blauert, Campilan, D., Gaventa, J. et al (eds) Learning from Change: Issues and experiences in participatory monitoring and evaluation. London: Intermediate Technology Publications Ltd. Pp.1-14.

" Feuerstein, M-T. (1986) Partners in Evaluation: Evaluating Development Community Programmes with Participants. London: MacMillan.

" Brisolara, S. (1998) 'The history of participatory evaluation and current debates in the field.' In Whitmore, E. (ed.) (1998) Understanding and Practicing Participatory Evaluation. New Directions for Evaluation, Number San Francisco: Jossey-Bass Publishers. Pp.25-41.

" Patton, M.Q. (1997a) Utilization-Focused Evaluation. Thousand Oaks, California: Sage Publications; Mark, M.M. and Shortland, R.L. (1985) Stake-holder-based Evaluation and value judgments: The role of perceived power and legitimacy in the selection of stakeholder groups.' Evaluation Review, 9, pp.605-626; Patton, M. Q. (1997b) 'Toward distinguishing empowerment evaluation and placing it in a larger context,' Evaluation Practice, 18 (2), 147-163.

" Cousins, J.B. and Whitmore, E. (1998) 'Framing Participatory Evaluation.' In Whitmore, E. (ed.) (1998) Understanding and Practicing Participatory Evaluation. New Directions for Evaluation, Number 80.

" Francisco: Jossey-Bass Publishers. Pp.5-23.

" Fetterman, D.M. (2001) Foundations of Empowerment Evaluation. Thousand Oaks: Sage Publications; McTaggart, R. (1991) 'When Democratic Evaluation doesn't seem democratic.' Evaluation Practice, 12(1), pp.9-21.

" Burke, B. (1998) op.cit.

" Aubel, J. (2004) Participatory Monitoring and Evaluation for Hygiene Improvement. Beyond the toolbox: What else is required for effective PM&E?

" Washington, D.C.: Environmental Health Project, Strategic Report 9.

" Cracknell, B.E. (2000) Evaluating Development Aid: Issues, Problems Solutions. Pp.110-111. New Delhi: Sage Publications; Kanji, N. (2003)

" Mind the Gap: Mainstreaming gender and participation in development. London: International Institute for Environment and Development (IIED) the Institute of Development Studies (IDS).

" Noponen, H. (1997) 'Participatory Monitoring and Evaluation - Prototype Internal Learning System for Livelihood and Micro-Credit Programs.' Community Development Journal, 32:1, pp.30-48 (p.47)

" Carden, F. (2000) 'Giving Evaluation Away: Challenges in a Learning based Approach to Institutional Assessment.' In Nair, K.S. and White, S.A. 1994) 'Participatory Development Communication as Cultural Renewal.'

" White, S.A. with Nair, K.S. and Ascroft, J. (eds) Participatory Communication: Working for change and development. New Delhi: Sage Publications. Pp.175-200.

" Whitmore, E. (ed.) (1998) Understanding and Practicing Participatory Evaluation. New Directions for Evaluation, Number 80. San Francisco: Jossey-Bass Publishers.

" Estrella, M. with Blauert, J., Campilan, D., Gaventa, J. et al (eds) (2000) Learning from Change: Issues and experiences in

Participatory Monitoring Evaluation. London: Intermediate Technology Publications Ltd.

" Cornwall, A. and Jewkes, R. (1995) 'What is participatory research?' Social Science & Medicine, 41 (12), 1667-1676; Roche, C. (1999) Methodological issues: using participatory tools.' In Impact Assessment for Development Agencies. Learning to Value Change. Oxford Publishing: Oxfam. 137-150.

" Feuerstein, M-T. (1986) Partners in Evaluation: Evaluating Development and Community Programmes with Participants. London: MacMillan; Chambers, R. (1991) 'Shortcut and Participatory Methods for Gaining Social Information for Projects.'

" In Putting People First: Sociological Variables in Rural Development. Cernea, M.M. (ed). Pp.515-537. Oxford: Oxford University Press; Narayan-Parker, D. (1993)

" Participatory evaluation: Tools for Managing Change in Water and Sanitation. World Bank Technical Paper 207. Washington, D.C.: The World Bank; MacMillan; Gajanayake, and Gajanayake, J. (1993)

" Community Empowerment: A Participatory Training manual on Community Project Development. Illinois: Office of International Training and Consultation, Northern Illinois University; Srinivasan, L. (1993) Tools for Community Participation: A Manual for Training Trainers in Participatory Techniques.

Media and Governance in a Democracy

Dr. Pooja Rana*

Social scientists of the liberal tradition have seen mass media as the Fourth Estate acting as a watchdog of the polity and its governance practices. Based on this tradition, mass media have been privileged to enjoy immunity from censorship of ideas and persecution and prosecution of the working journalists. Article 18 of the United Nations Declaration of Human Rights gives every citizen the right to freedom of thought, conscience and religion while Article 19 gives the right to freedom of opinion and expression and brooks no interference in the seeking, receiving and imparting of information and ideas through any media. Similarly, Article 19 in part 3 of the Indian constitution gives all citizens of India the Right to Freedom of Expression. Based on the recognition of the Right to Freedom of Expression, the liberal tradition derived the Right to Freedom of Press. The underlying assumption for this derivation has been the popularized belief that the mass media represents public opinion. As the custodian of the people's rights to speak freely and fearlessly, the media has zealously guarded any attempts at its suppression. This paper is an attempt to interrogate the premise of this derivation by analyzing the role played by mass media in good governance in a democratic political dispensation.

* Associate Professor,
Amity, Manesar

In the run-up to the fulfillment of this objective, we need to take a look at what we understand by good governance, the role of media in good governance as projected by the liberal tradition, its interrogation from the perspective of the Marxist tradition and a survey of the mass media studies in regard to their content and the extension of the public sphere.

What does good governance stand for?

Governance has been defined differently by different political commentators. Skirting past these definitions, we would like to define good governance as the efficient use of natural and human resources through effective systems and processes by an ever vigilant and visionary leadership for the greatest good of the greatest number of people without sacrificing the interests of the marginalized minority. This definition throws up the following ideational co-ordinates.

1. **Efficient use of natural and human resources:** every country is blessed with these two resources in varying degrees. Natural resources are limited. But the entire process of development is hinged on overcoming this limitation through the process of production that involves creation of new types of utilities from them. Through the creation of place and time utility, natural resources can be made available at places and periods of time where and when they are not normally available. Similarly, through the industrial process of production, new forms can be created from the original primary forms leading to the creation of form utility. The entire edifice of the secondary and tertiary sector of any economy stands on the infrastructure of the primary sector that includes agriculture and its allied activities and mining of minerals and metals. Similarly, the population of the country is also a human resource which contributes to its development as no economic activity can be undertaken by completely excluding human agency. Here again, the contribution of the human resource depends upon its values and ethics, its attitudes, its educational attainments and its skill-sets. Good governance involves the efficient use of natural

resources by adding value to them through production processes and efficient use of human resources by enhancing their competence and commitment to work. It, therefore, calls for three basic activities namely: inventory taking of the resources; adjudging of their quality and value addition.

2. **Putting in place effective systems and processes:** that the resources may be used efficiently, it is essential to put in place effective systems and processes of work. In administrative language, we could call them statutes, rules and regulations and in managerial language we could call them quality systems. The purpose of these systems and processes is to improve efficiency through the delineation of work flows that overcome obstructions and pilferages. As the overall purpose is to improve efficiency, the systems and processes should be flexible enough to adapt to the changing times. That is why there is a constant need for the review of existing rules and regulations and their modification from the standpoint of the efficiency of the system. The rules and regulations should at no time become an end in themselves. If they do, they tend to become obstructionists and breed corruption at all levels of governance. The engagement with effective systems and processes is vital for them to play an instrumental role in good governance.

3. **Ever vigilant and visionary leadership:** the leadership of the country should be ever vigilant to read the signs of change in both the internal and external environments. We live at a time when technology is getting obsolete at a rapid pace. Disruptive technologies render older forms of work and lifestyle redundant. At the same time, they open up new opportunities for growth and development. Many a times, these opportunities are not obvious. A visionary leadership seize the nascent opportunities in these technologies and reaps the harvest by taking the early bird initiative of optimally exploiting them. It is also important that the leadership should have commitment to its work for without commitment, it would not be able to accomplish either of the two.

4. **Prosperity of the majority:** good governance in a democratic set up must ensure that the gains of development do not remain restricted to a select few. These must percolate to the majority of the citizenry.

5. **Consideration for the minority:** the greatest good of the greatest number philosophy could be a disaster for minority groups in the population. In order that they are not left out of the developmental process, good governance must embrace the consideration for the minority groups as one of its cardinal virtues. In any country, there are always different kinds of minority groups. In the developmental process, particularly in a democracy, there is every likelihood of these minority groups being ignored. Good governance must ensure that in the pursuit of the majority interests, the interests of the minority do not get overlooked.

The Role of Media in Good Governance as per the Liberal Tradition

According to the liberal tradition, mass media represent public opinion. As the custodian of public's right to communicate, they act as public ombudsmen to oversee the functioning of the government through the frame of public perception and public good.

As per this instrumentalist view of the liberal tradition, mass media have a special responsibility to critique each of the domains of good governance, as given below:

Sl. No.	Good Governance	Role of Media
1.	Efficient use of natural and human resources inventory taking adjudging of their quality value addition	This requires the mass media to take a call on the manner in which the government of the day is taking care of the national resources and adding value to them by transforming primary goods into processed goods and training manpower to take on responsibilities that need intricate skills.
2.	Putting in place of effective systems and processes overcome obstructions and pilferages must serve a functional role	This requires the mass media to critique the statutes, rules and regulations in place and to assess their contemporary relevance and utility for facilitating citizen empowerment.
3.	Leadership Vigilant Visionary Committed	Mass media needs to assess the quality of national and regional leadership in terms of its competence and commitment.
4.	Prosperity of the majority	Mass media needs to interrogate the statistics given out by the government to assess the claims of its performance and to goad it to perform for the good of the citizens.
5.	Consideration for the minority	Mass media needs to verify if minority groups are not ignored and suggest ways and means of mainstreaming them in the life of the nation.

According to the liberal tradition of mass media theory, mass media plays all these roles adequately. But the Marxist tradition contests these claims. According to the Frankfurt School, mass media cannot play this glorified role as it is an industrial technology that thrives on the inaccessibility of the mediated public sphere to the citizen. The birth of industrial technologies made mass production of goods possible. As such, it was a beneficial move, but it also led to the concentration of wealth in the hands of those who got to own these technologies. This created asymmetries of power in the society. Mass media is no different from the industrial technologies. It restricts the access of the citizen to the mediated public sphere, apart from setting an agenda for debate and discussion as per its own convenience. As mass media is an economic activity involving huge investment in production technologies and distribution channels, mass media organizations look for returns on investments just as any other business organization does. The returns come primarily through advertising revenues with circulation figures acting as the pivot for higher ad revenues. The commercialization of mass media has had a direct fall out on its ability to sustain the public sphere. Instead, it has lead to the trivialization of its editorial content, apart from creating a unique situation where despite the mushroom growth of media organizations, the editorial content tends to display a unique uniformity. With mass media failing to live up to the ideal of the liberal tradition as the watchdog of the society and the mediated public sphere dissipating into a forum for the circulation of distorted information, gossip and inanities, mass media fails to critique good governance practices.

There are countless studies by communication experts on this failure of mass media despite enjoying immunity from all restrictions in the name of the citizen who has been granted the Right to Freedom of Expression by the Constitution. ArvindRajagopalin his edited book, The Indian Public Sphere: Readings in Media History, traces the emergence of the Indian public sphere right from the colonial times to the present day and shows therein how the mass media has never contributed to the development of a resilient and critical public sphere. Rajagopal clarifies that in the pre-indepence era, despite the emergence of print media, rumour was the strongest weapon of mobilization of the people. Similarly, in the post-independence era, despite the proliferation of the news channels, newspapers and magazines, radio stations and other mass media such as films, the public sphere has remained restricted to the urban middle class, in particular the upper caste Hindus, leaving out the majority of population comprising the other castes and communities as well as the economically depressed sections of the community.

Tracing the rise of the phenomenon of supplement journalism in post-liberalisedIndia, Pooja Rana remarks that despite breaking away from the pre-occupation with politics in the main paper, the content of newspaper supplements does not foster any meaningful dialogue on issues of public concern; instead the supplements churn out content that acts as bait for the advertisers. Besides, most of the subjects dealt with in supplements reflect the newspaper organizations' engagement with the cultural products consumed by the upper urban middle class Indian. The supplements create a media space in which the identity of the majority of Indians, who comprise around 94 per cent of the Indian population, is scarcely acknowledged. They also popularize the myth of a Shining India that the Arjun Sengupta Committee report debunks.

Apart from these studies, there are other studies which show that mass media in India shows signs of gullibility and collusion in its reportage. Studies show that most media organizations practice handout journalism in the sense that they report facts given out by the government without proper verifications of facts and figures, a lesson that every journalist learns as a part of the ABC of Journalism. The reason why the journalist fails to do so lies in the reluctance of the mass media to engage seriously with issues of common concern.

With the advertiser acting as the source of revenue, the newspaper can't help but dovetail all its space to his/her needs. Consequently, despite the proliferation of mass media in the country, the mass media has interrogated none of the constituents of good governance in India.

The Way out

The mass media leads us into a cul-de-sac, leaving us with no other option except the oral communication networks spoken of by ArvindRajagopal. But, just as satellite communication technology came as a godsend to break the stranglehold of the government on the freedom of the electronic media, rather television, to broadcast news, Internet has come as another disruptive technology to break the monopolistic control of the mass media over the public sphere. It started with journalists working for established newspapers in the USA and other developed countries starting their own blogs to circumvent the editorial gatekeeping of their respective papers. It continued with citizens wielding the cyber pen and churning millions of web logs in support of the problems faced by their respective communities. The recent upheavals in the Middle East and the early one in Indonesia concerning the freedom of East Timor Islands are cases in point. Nearer home the Mumbai serial blasts evoked a blast of discussion on usenet groups and discussion sites, demanding action on the ground from the government and alerting citizens to their rights and responsibilities.

The new media comes as a Saviour, plugging the gaps of the mass media and promising a new public sphere, which is democratic in spirit and action. As a communication technology, it has been hailed as a complete media. It integrates all the media born to date by blending the oral and the written text with the visual one. Besides, it is at once an interpersonal media technology like the telephone and a mass media technology like the television and the newspaper. Furthermore, even as a mass media technology, it does not monopolize the mediated public sphere by restricting access of the citizen to it. On the World Wide Web, anyone can post any information of any kind in the personal or public domain. So, one can upload a video or a series of videos on public networking sites such as the YouTube and attract attention of the world wide audience. At the same site, one can discuss the uploaded video.

The removal of restrictions on the mass broadcast of videos and the mass circulation of verbal texts on the web by the citizens fosters a new form of journalism which is not institutionalized like the mass media. In fact, it would be wrong to call it journalism of any kind. It would be more appropriate to call it as online communication. By empowering the citizen to participate in the public sphere, online communication invests the public sphere with the criticality that JurgenHabermas and Nacy Fraser spoke of in their respective works.

The caveat to this role is the increasing attempts of governments in different countries to muzzle the freedom of netizens to express themselves on the Net and that of corporate organizations to control and monitor the flow of information on the web. China has devised its own search engines but also heavily guarded and filtered the flow of information on the Internet. So, have some of the despotic governments in the Middle East. But, this evil is not restricted to these kinds of governments alone. Even the USA, the champion of freedom of conscience and free speech, has been regulating the content on the web ever since it was born. The infamous Carnivore and ECHELON are cases in point of state surveillance in the US. Govt of India has also come out with an IT Act, which has the explicit aim of facilitating the use of Internet for e-commerce and the implicit purpose of snooping on the Internet. Studies by PavanDuggal, cyber law expert, show that there are a number of provisions in the Act which are not citizen friendly. The other threat comes from the corporate organizations which have always tried to kill any communication technology that facilitates the access of the citizen to information reception and production. One of the strongest weapons in their kitty has been the issue of 'copyright'. In a recent meeting of the Internet Society, James Barlow questioned the right of the copyright owners to arrest the flow of information on the World Wide Web as he found it not only motivated by profiteering but also by the desire to muzzle the growth of peer networks. He found all these attempts as anti-democratic in spirit and therefore worthy of being questioned and abjured.

One other caveat to the re-energisation of the modern public sphere is the digital divide. It creates a new class of outcastes, the digital outcastes. Though the access of this class to the new media is going to be greatly facilitated by the introduction of 3G services in cell phones, it will still remain an area of concern as long as the cell phone prices do not fall well within their reach. At the same time, we need to understand that the new media technology is still in the process of evolution. Future developments in this technology promise to bring greater relief to this section of the population. Innovations at MIT by Prof Mistry raise these hopes.

So, we conclude that while the mass media could not fructify the hope of a public sphere which could enforce good governance practices, new media has raised hopes of the emergence of a public sphere which can be both inclusive and critical of aberrations and corruptions in governance practices, subject of course to regulatory controls and attempts at corporatization of the internet.

Bibliography

Coronel, Sheila; Corruption and the Watchdog Role of the News Media

http://www.humanrights.com/what-are-human-rights/universal-declaration-of-human-rights.html

Roosevelt, Eleanor; Human Rights: United Nations Declaration (audio CD)

Chaturvedi, Patanjali Nandan; The United Nations and the Human Rights

State University Of New York Press (2006); Governance and the Public Good

Mander, Harsh; Good Governance

Sardar, N.K. & Mujawar, W.R.; Democracy Good Governance And Human Rights

Rajagopalachari, C; Words Of Freedom: Ideas Of A Nation

gseis.ucla.edu/faculty/kellner/papers/fs.htm?

http://media.illinois.edu/images/_docs/Chapter7.pdf

http://people.bath.ac.uk/hssbpn/theories%20of%20media.htm

Sen, Amartya; Peace and Democratic Society

Rajagopal, Arvind; The Indian Public Sphere Readings in Media History

Rana, Pooja; Supplement Journalism in India

Habermas,Jurgen; The Structural Transformation of the Public Sphere

http://www.hks.harvard.edu/fs/pnorris/Acrobat/WorldBank Report/Chapter%205%20Coronel.pdfhttp://www.hks.harvard.edu/fs/pnorris/Acrobat/WorldBankReport/Chapter%205%20Coronel.pdf

Impact of Television on Children Psyche with Special Reference to Cartoon Channels

Parul Malhotra*

Abstract

Television is an audio-visual and sophisticated scientific device. It telecasts programmes from far and wide areas of the country and abroad. Amongst all the mass media today, television attracts the largest number of viewers. This is because television is able to attract the audiences of all age groups, literate and illiterate and of all the strata of the society. In the last three decades the growth of television both in technology and reach has been phenomenal. Television as a mass medium informs, educates, inspires and motivates.

Television can be a powerful influence in developing value systems and behaviour in children. Television may be a socializing force but it interacts in composite ways with all of the other forces in a child's life to determine the patterns of socialization of the child. Nobody can deny that children, to an extent, learn about fashion, language, compliance, social exchanges, values, principles and a whole host of behavioral patterns from viewing television As most children spend more time engaged in television viewing especially cartoons

Assistant Professor
Department of Journalism and Mass Communication
JIMS, Rohini-3, Delhi-110085

than in any other single activity besides school, its impact on their learning social and affective development cannot be over looked. Children spend more time on watching cartoons and acquiring much information not only about type of cartoon characters but also they are familiar with the action, dress and name of almost all major cartoon characters. Children are at a stage where their minds are developing and form impressions very easily. At such an early stage children consider the things they watch in cartoons to be real, they are unable to differentiate between fantasy and reality

This research article offers an overview of the Impact of Television on Children Psyche with special reference to Cartoon Channels

Key words: Television, Children, Cartoon channels, Psyche

1. Introduction

Amongst all the mass media today, television attracts the largest number of viewers. It has an important role to play for entertainment and education of people all over the world. It is the most commonly found electronic appliance in every household. Almost all individuals especially children are exposed to it some or the other time. Television may be a socializing force for everyone but it interacts in various ways with all of the other forces in a child's life. Studies have shown that children are among the heaviest users of television. Young children usually spend between 3 and 4 hours watching television each day. They are mostly affected by the cartoons which are their favorites. Nobody can deny the fact that cartoons are favorite of most of the children.

2. Objective

The objective of this paper is to find out the impact of television on children psyche with special reference to cartoon channels.

3. Research Methodology

Research is secondary in nature. It includes the review of various research papers, articles and internet.

4. Conceptual Discussion

4.1 Role of Television

Television is an audio-visual and sophisticated scientific device. It telecasts programmes from far and wide areas of the country and abroad. Amongst all the mass media today, television attracts the largest number of viewers. It has an important role to play for entertainment and education of people all over the world. Its audience is greater in size than any of the other media audiences. This is because television is able to attract the audiences of all age groups, literate and illiterate and of all the strata of the society. Various programmes on television represent various religions and cultural expressions and activities of people, belonging to different parts of India, thus it reflects the Indian society.

In India, from the beginning i.e. 1989, television has been used more for education and information purposes than for entertainment. It has performed different functions as compared to the television in west. Dr. Rajendra Prasad, while inaugurating India's Television Service on September 15, 1959, hoped that television would go a long way in broadening the people's outlook with scientific thinking. Television in India, through its programmes presents a composite national picture and perspective of India's rich cultural heritage and diverse thinking. In the last three decades the growth of television both in technology and reach has been phenomenal. Its role as an important communication medium is noteworthy for promoting national unity, developing economy and refining socio-cultural life of people.

Television, being an audio-visual medium, brings us into contact with events in an exciting and clarifying way. Television has more flexibility and mobility in its coverage due to audio-visual presentation. This is the reason why it has become a family medium. Family members receive messages in their own environment. As far as educational messages to the masses are concerned, television is the most powerful educational medium because it combines speaking, writing and showing. You not only talk to the masses at one time but you show them what you mean. Thus, TV presents mass demonstration to thousands of viewers at the same time.

Televisions' another function is to provide entertainment to people. It has become the most common source of entertainment recently. It offers many types of amusements to the viewers - comedy, action and drama are some of the most popular amusements. Action entertainment offers thrillers, suspense, crime, investigation and police shows. There are more entertainment programmes like musical shows and movies videos on MTV, VTV, UTV Bindaas and others. Movie channels like HBO and star movies broadcast popular movies. Animated cartoon shows for children are very popular where famous characters make children laugh. TV has indeed occupied its place in every household by becoming the common entertainment.

4.2 Television and Children

Television can be a powerful influence in developing value systems and behaviour in children. It has brought about a substantial change in the experience of childhood in our culture. Any change in the behaviour and value systems of children will in turn change the future of society. In this sense, it can be seen that the television is shaping society. Television has great impact on various aspects of a child's life. It is a matter of great concern to educationists, planners, psychologists and pediatricians' world over. Television viewing enhances cognitive development, and conveys knowledge, skills and information to the child. It motivates learning and imparts general awareness. It promotes both conceptual and concrete thinking, and helps in bringing change in behavior and attitudes.

However, television viewing has negative effects too. It may place children in inactive roles. It may provide escapism from reading, playing, exercise, study etc. It decreases actual social interaction, and provides antisocial or aggressive and destructive roles for imitation.

Since it came into our homes, television became the subject of many debates, citizens' actions, and network responses because of possible impact on children psyche. Several researches have been done in mid-twentieth to investigate and possibly prove the impact of television on children psyche.

Of course, TV in control can be a good thing: Preschoolers can get help learning the alphabet on public television, primary school goers can learn about wildlife, nature, art and craft, culture, tradition through various shows, and parents can keep up with current events on the evening news. No doubt TV can be an excellent educator and entertainer, but the negative side of it cannot be ignored. The first 2 years of life are considered a critical time for brain development. TV and other electronic media can get in the way of exploring, playing, and interacting with parents and others, which encourages learning and healthy physical, cognitive and social development.

As kids get older, too much TV time can get in the way with activities such as being physically active, reading, writing, doing homework, playing with friends and spending time with family

Watching TV for children has both positive and negative effects. First, I will talk about the positive effects:

" It helps child to collect his lessons by watching educational television programs.

" Get as much information and the formation of a cultural character by watching cultural programs.

" Identify the different types of art and various forms of music.

" Spend more time with the family to watch television programs and discussed.

The negative effects are

" Children who watch TV for long hours they probably will have negative impacts on their health such as they may weak their eye-sight at young age.

- Changes their behavior: Children may change their behavior toward other people. Many children tend to follow their favorite actors or actress and imitate them by wearing same cloths, following same attitude and try to speak same languages.
- Waste time
- Viewing action films increases aggressive behavior and violence to the child.
- Watching television for long hours of the most important causes of obesity in children.
- TV ads affect the child and make him eat the fast foods which are harmful to health.
- TV develops some wrong behaviors of the child, such as: smoking, addiction, and the use of violence as a means to get what he wants.

4.3 Cartoon Channels and Children

Cartoons are a main source of entertainment for children. Children keenly observe the actions of cartoons. Have you ever met any children who do not like cartoons? Or have you ever seen any children who refuse to watch cartoon? This situation is mostly impossible under normal circumstances. Before mentioning the effects of cartoon channels or cartoons on children, I would like to talk about the reasons that why children watch cartoons.

First of all, the basic reason for children's watching cartoons is that a cartoon can satisfy children's desire to entertain. Children watch cartoons for fun and entertainment. They find cartoon characters funny and amusing. Secondly, cartoons respond to the children's need and liking to activeness. Mostly the children under the age of seven are so much interested in cartoons. They think that whatever happens in cartoons are all real and they can do everything that the characters in cartoons do. Thirdly, cartoons act as temporary partners of children. They firstly watch cartoons and then imitate them. They are prone to take cartoons as their models and reflect the characters in their daily games.

Children watch cartoons for entertainment. They prefer those cartoons which are understandable in terms of language. When children see cartoons in easy and understandable language, they enjoy more, and are involved more. Cartoons are the most frequent and easily accessible source of entertainment which we provide to our children. There is a wide range of cartoons from fairy tales like 'Beauty and the Beast', Doremon, Shinchan to action-based cartoons like 'Ben Ten' and 'Pokémon' It has become easier for children to watch their favourite cartoons with the vastness of media and extension of channels, on a single click and at the same time it has become more convenient for parents to provide children with this all-time favourite activity of theirs. Children spend more time on watching cartoons and acquiring much information not only about type of cartoon characters but also they are familiar with the action, dress and name of almost all major cartoon characters.

Indian animated channels gained new level in Indian television broadcast with the emergence of international animation channels and numerous national channels. Earlier, before the emergence of satellite television, only Doordarshan used to telecast cartoons and animated shows for the Indian audience, particularly kids. But with the arrival of Cartoon Network in the year 1995, popular animated shows and cartoons were presented to the viewers for the first time. Eventually lot more animated channels, international and national, started to come up in India. Now there are a number of Animation Channels that offers various types of programmes from cartoons, shows related to games, art and crafts like Disney channel, Hungama channel, Cartoon Network, Pogo etc. Many popular animated and kids` movies are also premiered on these channels, some even dubbed in Hindi and other regional languages

Round the clock cartoons are on air on Cartoon channels. Because of this, we can see desolate playgrounds and children's casual attitude towards studies. Earlier children used to spend their leisure time in outdoor activities but nowadays they can be found glued to the TV sets for long hours, watching all sorts of cartoons, mostly without the supervision of elders who are completely unaware that this might have certain effects on their physical and psychological development later on displayed in their behavior patterns. Children are at a stage where their minds are developing and form impressions very easily. At such an early stage children consider the things they watch in cartoons to be real, they are unable to differentiate between fantasy and reality, so parents need to be careful to what their children are exposed to.

No doubt watching cartoons have become a point of worry for parents especially working parents. Nowadays, society has changed a lot. Most parents work, so they do not have enough time to be with their children and play with them for most of the day. Automatically many children play by themselves, and most of them spend time watching cartoons on the television. Parents cannot keep track of what their children are watching as most of the time they are not at home. Yet, most parents do not let their children watch cartoons too much because they get worried about the effects of cartoons on their children. If their children watch cartoons too much, it could affect their eyes. It will not damage their eyes, but rather will result in eye fatigue. Even though most children know that watching television is bad for their eyes, they still watch cartoons on television from a close distance. That is why many children are wearing glasses these days.

Watching cartoons also results in losing the attention span. While children are watching the cartoons, the screen changes many times every second, which is not good for the child because of the screen is doing all of the thinking for the child, so it is very hard to improve children's imagination. This may be the reason that why most people call the television an idiot box. Children learn lots of things about the world from television, especially in cartoons, in the early years of their life. As we know, Cartoons have a huge influence on children. Most cartoons are series, so if the child likes that particular series, they watch it almost every day because they are addicted to that cartoon. While children are watching cartoons, they do not think deeply but after watching it, they still remember the story and also they think that story is a part of their life. This is affecting the creativity of children.

Most children are likely to imitate what they see on television because children tend to think that most famous cartoon characters are heroes, so they want to act and speak like them. If a main character steals and uses other people's belongings then children imitate that behaviour and they may think it is right. They do not learn good habits naturally so it could bring problems in their moral sense. It is frequently seen in the cartoon shows that the cartoon characters commit crime and don't get punished. Children take it for granted and are unable to distinguish between the reel and real. They do not know that such things do not exist in the real world.

Parents are also worried about mental and emotional problems with their children, which could come from watching violent cartoons. These days, there are lots of violent cartoons, and children are getting aggressive because if they see very bad behaviour in cartoons, they just imitate that action. Three major effects have been proven by psychological research caused by children seeing violence on television are that the child may become less sensitive to the pain and suffering of others; children who watch violence do not fear violence nor are they bothered by violence in general and the children are more likely to become aggressive or use harmful actions towards others. They accept the violence as a way to solve the problems as beating each other is very commonly seen in cartoons.

But it's not that cartoons have only negative effects on children. Cartoons are the central focus of many children's lives that parents manipulatively use to help keep the children engaged while they are busy with their office schedules. Children at every age learn a variety of things easily by watching educational cartoon films like 'Krishna', 'Ramayan', 'Hanuman' and 'Chota Bheem'. They inculcate religious values and teach children about Indian mythology. Infants and toddlers start learning different words, and their meanings. Also, cartoons have a tremendous impact in improving the cognitive aspects among young children. Children become more creative by watching cartoons. Cartoons provide children with the related social and self-knowledge. They try to do things in different ways so their imagination and creativity is enhanced. There are lots of cartoons, which are not only the best source of entertainment, but could also be used for educational purposes. For instance, cartoons like 'Dora the Explorer' can be used for some brain activity making children learning shapes or identify colors etc.

Cartoon shows are neither good nor bad .Watching Cartoons for children has both positive and negative effects. First I will talk about positive points.

" Occasionally cartoons are being used to demonstrate behavior that we would like our young children to adapt or copy, and even many times these cartoon shows are also used to exemplify qualities we would like our kids to avoid. It is up to the parents to help the child learn which is which.

" From time to time there have been some good series like Madeline, Oswald, Noddy, Backyard Science, MAD, Mickey Mouse Club House. And some Hindi Indian Cartoons, which I would suggest are Gali Gali Sim Sim, Choota Bheem, Krishna, Ramayan and all Mythological stories.

" It helps improve vocabulary; it could be English or Hindi. It helps kids in analyzing situations. To understand how small little things are analyzed and then how small little decisions are taken by understanding what is right and wrong. It helps them understand different cultures, societies, people etc.

" There are so many shows, which are really educational, for all ages. And some programs show various Art and Craft activities, which can be actually utilized to put them to some creative work.

The negative points are:

" With the kids watching television all the time, their physical activities which can only be achieved by playing in a playground are not taken care of.

" Kids try to imitate what they see on television. Be it language or violence, they just want to behave like their "Super Hero".

" When parents continually leave their children to be entertained by the television it can have negative effects on child's mind because children are primarily proactive and like to be doing something.

" And one of the major concerns is the time kids spent in watching those cartoons. Every mother has a tough time moving her kids away from television. Ideally what I would suggest is to have fixed television-watching timings.

5. Conclusion

It has been indicated through this article that watching cartoons is already a habit for most children, and it has become a part of their lives. They tend to imitate whatever they see in cartoons as they are unable to comprehend the difference between fact and fantasy or right and wrong. This is a very risky situation not only for mental development of the children but also for their perceptions in all aspects.

Parents should think about how to prevent their children from the bad effects of cartoons. First of all, parents should spend time with their kids as much as they can. If they do not have enough time to spend with their children, they should know that what kind of cartoons their children watch every day. It's extremely significant that parents should follow what kind of cartoons their children watch. If parents think that the cartoon is not appropriate for their child, they should not allow them to watch that cartoon anymore, and instead, let them read books and play other games, which would help children in their mental and physical growth.

Parents should choose the most beneficial cartoons that will not only entertain the children but also give appropriate messages to them. All these cartoons are adaptations from children's classics which aim to develop children mentally. For e.g. 'Dora the explorer', Mickey mouse. Tom and Jerry or any other cartoon related to mythological characters.

The influence of cartoons can be made positive by a little effort on the part of parents or elders. They should make their kids realize that these fantasy things have no true value and identity, no such 'Spiderman' exists who will jump from top of one building to another with the help of his web or there is no such 'Ben 10' wristwatch which will start blinking and will alert Ben of every evil action before hand. If someone is killed or beaten up by cartoons it does not mean that kids should also start doing the same. Parents need to keep an eye on their children's activities and should be observant of any peculiar changes in their behavior. With intervals they should interrogate them and try to clear the reality of things and should answer the controversial and ambiguous questions they have in their mind. Thus, for making cartoons a healthy entertainment and a good and effective source of learning for children parents should pay a little attention towards providing selective cartoons to their children which could have a positive impact on them.

6. References:

1. Dowshen Steven, How TV affects your child. Retrieved from kids health: www.kidshealth.org
2. Tandon Anisha, Impact of Cartoons on Children. Retrieved from study mode: www.studymode.com

3. Patel Ismail Adam, March 26, 2008, The effects of Television on children, Riyadul Jannah online Volume: 2/Issue: 7
4. Nawaz Muhammad, Bakht Mahsud, Yaser RawanNoman, Spring 2009, The effects of tv cartoon network on the aggressive behavior of school going children, Global Media Journal online volume II, Issue 1
5. B.Kadam Prashant, Bhosale Ashwini S. and Bagala Ashwini, A study on effects of cartoon networks (television) on children. Indian Streams Research Journal Vol.2,Issue.IV/May; 12
6. Gupta R.K., Saini D.P., Acharya U. and Miglani N, Impact of Television on Children, Indian J Pediatr 1994; 61 : 153-159
7. Sampat Malvika, How Good Or Bad Are Cartoon Channels For Your Kids? Retrieved from ezine articles: www.ezinearticles.com
8. Bibi Alia and Zehra Roshan, Effects of cartoons on children's psychology & behaviour patterns. Retrieved from the news: www.thenews.com.pk
9. Choma C.J., Hossle Stevie, Leu Robert, Ray DiviNelson Shawnte, Wilcox Ben, Ybarra Brandon, Effects of Cartoons on Children. Retrieved from bgsu: www.bgsu.edu
10. Swastik, what is the role of Television in Education? Retrieved from preserve articles: www.preservearticles.com
11. Payal Kamat, Television as Mass Medium. Retrieved from preserve articles: www.preservearticles.com
12. Anonymous, the Role and Influence of Mass Media. Retrieved from Cliff Notes: www.cliffnotes.com
13. Anonymous, Cartoons and their effects on children. Retrieved from Word press: www.wordpress.com
14. Anonymous, The Emotional Effects of cartoons on children. Retrieved from Life style- Sulekha: www.sulekha.com

North-East in Media: Representation vs. Reality

Payel Chakrabarti* and Liza Das**

Abstract

Northeast India has always been represented in media in violent images, usually through stereotypical projection. And moreover the region is believed to have been denied due space and time in the so called mainstream media. To grab quick attention, events with sensational images are mostly represented, which create negative impact of the region and people among a wider audience. Through media representation the positive identity and positive impression about a particular person place or event, should be communicated rather than reinforcing prejudices and emphasising stereotypes. Over time it is seen that most of the incidents of violence in the Northeast have attracted media attention. Content analyses proves that media text on and from the Northeast mostly tend to define the region as per the saleable value of news content which reinforce the prejudiced perceptions leading to even stronger perception creation.

This paper examines the current functioning of media in portraying the region and specifically deals with patterned projection of Northeast India and studies the role of media to project motivating images of the local being. It looks into few selected

*Research Scholar, **Associate Professor
Department of Humanities and Social Sciences, IIT Guwahati, Guwahati-781039

instances of representation of northeast in news and how it affects the local imaging based on a survey on local respondent's perceptions and aspirations. Students from selected academic institutions (representing local as well and nationwide views) of Guwahati and media industry representatives' views were taken into consideration to figure out the present state of the region and the reflected reality in media. This calls for relooking into the media format of stereotypical projection of the region that has been neglecting many other facets of reality.

Keywords: Media representation, patterned projection, Northeast perception.

Introduction

The projection of the north-eastern region and its people in the media may be said to be in sync with the 'popular culture' which cannot be taken as complete reality. Over time it is seen that most the incidents of violence in the Northeast which have attracted media attention (mainstream as well as locals) are understood to be either politically charged; or are by some militant or ethnic group to either grab attention, show strength, sustenance and growth or to scare people and government. Violence featured in media are mostly politically motivated violence such as demonstrations, arsons, riots, and clashes with police etc which affect a larger section of masses, rather than those of crime. As violence has more news and visual value, often political and extremist groups resort to violence to get noticed by mass media (Gupta, 2006).

It is also seen that representations in media of northeast mostly revolve around the issue relating to ethnic identity which the media has been highlighting in certain negative light focusing on the violence. Content analysis proves that media texts on Northeast India define the region as bomb blasts, terrorism, infiltration and tribes. "Political violence- murders, bombings, kidnappings, extortions militants, killing of militants by security forces in actual or staged encounters¬ has become a routine part of news from the Northeast" (Baruah, 2005). If not for out of control massacres, riots, curfews, agitations and other incidents of violence eruption, Northeast remains unnoticed and neglected (Hazarika, 1994). Such coverages which have over the time proved to be very money-making as well as well-accepted are report stories about acts of violence and Northeast is used as a fertile plot for such marketisation.

A certain kind of reports only get projected, whereas various other aspects which may be important, like perception of ethnic lifestyle identity, myriad tradition and cultural heterogenic harmony and aspiration towards future, are neglected by media (Chakrabarti 2011). It is seen that many incidents go unnoticed by the media, many are misreported, many denied coverage branding it to be less important compared to news from mainland India and incidents are only covered that fit into the existing set of prejudices regarding the region, which are again self created by media itself. That's why it can be in a way justified to call the northeastern part of the country 'paradise in peril'. And as these have become the only projected issues outside the region, even though the media cannot be always blamed for providing the bias; but many a times the media can be held responsible for stirring up the prejudices that lie deep within people. The prejudiced perceptions, about the region as being disturbed and situations frightening, are further reinforced by media leading to even stronger perception creation. As a result people living outside these regions have a mediated and largely distorted picture of the region and the people.

Extensive isolation and neglect mainly due to location and poor connectivity with the rest of India have all played a part in creating this scenario and generating the perception. Many believe the region lacks the sense of belonging and inclusive national identity. Similarly, with the emphasis on violence, conflict, and projection of white male prime-of-life power, media consumers develop a sense of denial. Viewer sections who find neglected place in media or minorities in media who see members of their own group underrepresented but overvictimised develop a greater sense of apprehension, mistrust, and alienation (Kamalipour and Rampal, 2001). This holds true for the Northeastern region as well. For example ethnic separatists movements have affected Assam, Manipur, Mizoram and Nagaland to a large extent. These, similar to the movements occurred in Kashmir and Punjab, are only different in the sense that Northeastern movements have not received media attention like the others. (Baruah, 1999).

The region gets least projected in the mainstream media and whatever little is adopted by the media are very selective aspects of the region mostly focusing on the identity and ethnicity issues clubbed with conflict and violence. Local media of the region have also not been able to satisfy the needs of the region and the people in improving the media scenario. Numerous incidents of human rights violation on the various indigenous people happen without being known to the outside world because of inaccessibility of the region and backwardness particularly in media world (Biswas and Thomas, 2006). Mainland media of India has often looked at the Northeast as perennially disturbed area with focus on either Indian security concerns or militant activities launched by various ethnic or extremist groups. In long run it has been seen that the concern is about the insecurity and acts of violence and not about the people. Big media houses have no time and space to report about the people who despite adverse situation (if any) are still coping up with them (Singh, 1998). Of the causes of violence in the state of Assam, as cited by various respondents in a study undertaken by North-Eastern Students' National Integration Movement in 2001 to 2005, it was found that media influence and feeling of hurt and rejection figure as influencing factors (Kallarackal, 2007). It is seen that it is only the understanding of the region to be underdeveloped, economically backward and at the same time detached with the mainstream India; is what makes the disorders of the region durable; put as "lends legitimacy to today's durable disorders" (Baruah, 2005).

Role played by media has been enormous in shaping up Northeast to what it is today (Baruah, 2005). Various media intrusions into the political in social scenario are affecting the people and the region as a whole and even outside the boundaries. These include representations in stereotypical manner of brutality, extremism, emphasising certain ideologies etc which in many cases might be different from what it was expected to be like; and branding most of the conflicts of the region as ethnic. The role of media in the region along with many other parts needs to be redefined, if the media in Northeast needs to function for the wellbeing of the society or for dissemination and promotion of ideologies or for disseminating terror in the region and about the region outside. It draws attention to look into the ground realities, what is being projected by media and how much of it is justified.

Projection Vs. reality- the role of media marketisation

The present situation in terms of media representations can be said to be only selective and patterned which is basically due to the pertinent commercial attitude (Chakrabarti and Das, 2012). In case of Northeast the discriminatory behaviour of the mainstream media can be seen on the way representations of the region in media has been restricted to specific issues and nature. With marketisation of news, and constant patterned representation of violence from and of the region, news from the region has become more of a negatively advertised product. Thus it becomes important to study the effectiveness and appropriateness in various mass scale productions of homogeneous media products.

The issue that has often escaped academicians and industry is that how far is media being used as a medium to communicate reality and how much is to earn TRPs only; and if at all it is being used as communication with commercial gains, is it justifiable to give in to the aspirations of individuals or groups to gain TRPs at the cost of the identity of the whole region and its people. It needs to be re-looked into whether the media representations really go along with aspirations and life philosophy of the locals; how much of what is shared to the other parts of country and beyond is the true prevalent picture. The role of media highly plays significant in defining the region, mainstream attention towards only saleable sensational issues from Northeast (national as well as local media) only results in not-so-true Northeast being defined to media consumers, masses.

This paper is combination of views on representation of violence in media with the opinions expressed by the media expects and the media users, comprising both locals and non-locals, even residents and non-residents of the region from both the said groups. It deals with patterned projection of Northeast in media and studies the role of media to project motivating images of the local being. It looks into few selected instances of representation of northeast in news and how it affects the local imaging based on a survey on local respondent's perceptions in one hand and aspirations on the other. Students from selected academic institutions of Guwahati and media industry representatives' views were taken into consideration to figure out the present state of the region and the reflected reality in media. This transparent a need to relook into the media format of stereotypical projection of the region, that has been neglecting many other facets of reality.

Northeast and perception creation by media

To understand the prevailing media scenario and the motivating factors behind it, selective experts responded giving the following view that reflect Northeast in general and Assam in particular have been represented in media in a manner which is in a way not similar to the representation of the rest of the parts of India even during similar cases. Below are some instances which emerged while interacting with the respondents and referring to some of their writings.

Example 1: Mumbai blasts coverage and Guwahati blasts coverage

Media especially news channels in Mumbai blasts case for the first two days were just reporting the event. But from the third day there were feature stories talking about gaining back of strength and confidence and fighting back. More or less news headlines were like "Mumbai coming back to normalcy". Now in the case of Guwahati the blasts were reported as it is for the initial days and then there were no follow up stories. And so there was no gaining back of power to normalcy. Even if the local news media tried to do something of that kind as continuous follow ups for a few days the national media ignored the later parts. This is only one instance, but repeated incidents of similar nature and different kinds of media coverage, has facilitated creation of strong perceptions regarding different media treatment about different places facing similar incidents. While Mumbai is understood to be a city which never gives up, Assam is perceived by and large as a terror stricken state.

Example 2: DY365 channel

"Enough is enough. Editorial desk of DY--365 has decided not to telecast any news of Bandh call in future." stated a social networking post by the channel. DY 365, a satellite channel from Assam, had recently taken a decision of not airing any news of Bandh (strikes) in the state. This came after the High Court verdict of illegal bandhs. Here raises the question can the national media also not exercise these kinds of selective omissions in order to generate and maintain peace in the region and also to propagate a better positive image to the rest of the world outside the region. The media can atleast take stand to showcase the steps taken by the administration to maintain normalcy and also do proper follow up stories regarding unrestful situations.

Example 3: Doordarshan vs. private players

News content analysis of the news channels shows that while Doordarshan Northeast (public service broadcaster) portrays variety in their programmes. But other news channels focus on issues like that of violence to grab easy attention. The reason behind this was said to be the non profit motive of Doordarshan being a public broadcaster by the respondents. On the other hand the highly maintained profit margin of the private owned news channels define the news content which is more or less maintaining prejudiced facts of the region being disturbed.

Citation that clarifies conflict

Some facts which never really get highlighted in media include positive news, services and scopes that the region has in contributing towards development of the nation as a whole. As per facts the northeast is important to India because it is rich in oil, tea, paddy, timber, water and minerals. Assam supplies about 25 per cent of India's scarce indigenous oil. The massive Brahmaputra River flows though it and has carved out a large, fertile river valley. This is a classic case of a resource-rich sub-region dominated by a political heartland that is ethnically, and in many cases religiously, different. This perceived resource exploitation has even contributed to some of the separatist movements in recent years. But what is to be noticed is media seldom does portray the recourses but rather focuses on the conflicts that the resources lead to at times. Thus it is essential to answer every myth and lie; encounter every wrong signal- emanating even from the governments' wrong actions; and propaganda of the insurgents and the media supporting them in regard to the northeastern region. There is a need of an all out frontal intellectual war with a view to eliminating confusions and haziness of ideas. The conscientious citizens, the civil society forums and the media should play a positive role (Kumara, 2007).

Experts even believe it is the media representations only which even led to further confusions and distrust among the people, leading to further conflicts. As it is that these are because of the population mix and the very high emotions that run through because of factors political n social (said by Assam DGP Jayanta Choudhury in an interview on a national television channel). This is what in turn gets reflected and reinforced in the media consumers as well far and wide.

As put forth by Chetan Bhagat in one of his articles talking about his own experiences of the region Northeast, most of the youth respondents also echo a similar point of view. There is a subtle appeal for attention and being taken as a part of India and not outsiders. And this neglected feeing is generated and reconfirmed by the media space and content. Northeast has been in the news for the wrong reasons, many in the region feels the same. But unfortunately the media is yet to accept the fact that northeast deserves a rightful place in the media map as well along with its place in other fields.

In realising what the media has been doing to the mindsets of the people outside the region this next instance is worth mention. "I expected to be greeted by guns and was sure of getting killed by a stray bullet" had reflected Smita Agnihotri, Deputy Financial Adviser of North East Frontier Railway talking about her initial fear of being transferred to Assam. An official of the Indian Railway Service, like many others, she had a stereotypical notion of the northeastern region. Later residing in the region and getting to know the actual scenario which was actually not so grin she later wrote in an online web article, people outside the region do tend to fearfully avoid the region and "it is because encouraging facets about the region never get discussed by the media". This distorted view is perpetrated by the media which reports more on discontent and militant activities, than the region's uniqueness.

Pamela Philipose, Guest Editor of an online portal The Thumb Print, feels that the media in the Northeast are important as they are the only means to hold up a mirror to the region and reflect it to the world beyond, a unique story in itself which holds up a mirror to India and reflects the country's contradictions and strengths, the country's historical transgressions and future expectations. She states that it is essential to "challenge the way the largely Delhi-centric mainstream media defines India, decide news priorities and capture contemporary realities."

In today's context the words 'The true function of journalism is to educate the public mind, not to stock it with wanted and unwanted impressions' of M. K. Gandhi is very much relevant; we need to take note of it keeping aside all other motives behind factual representation.

People groups who opined their views when contacted

Based in Guwahati, four selected regional television channels - News Live, DY 365, Frontier TV and Doordarshan Northeast; and four newspapers- *The Telegraph, The Times of India, The Sentinel* and *The Sevensisters Post*, have been surveyed. The television channels are selected based on highest viewership among the rest of the regional channels of Assam. Whereas *The Telegraph* and *The Times of India* are national news dailies having regional editions, *The Sentinel* and *The Sevensisters Post* are regional newspapers, all published in English are selected with circulation even outside Assam so that responses would be not confined to local views and aspirations. From the industry, respondents were interviewed from each media house (4 television channels and 4 newspapers).

Views from youth were gathered from students of Handique Girls College, Assam Engineering Institute, Girls Polytechnic College, as local representation, where 30 students in each institution were met with specific purpose of getting their expressions about their perception of life experience and expectations; group of students from Indian Institute of Hotel Management Guwahati, Guwahati Medical College, Tezpur University and random selection from time to time of students across IIT Guwahati as national representation were selected.

Six academicians (faculty members 3 from each institute) from IIT Guwahati, Tezpur University; and 14 local people engaged in different occupations, were chosen randomly in and around Guwahati as and when scopes emerged to take up the matter, were individually spoken to as part of the survey. And views of experts including Pamela Philipose, Guest Editor, *The Thumb Print*; Indrani Raimedhi, Freelance Writer; Teresa Rehman, Editor *The Thumb Print*; Bhaswati Khaund Centre for Northeast studies, Delhi University; Sanjoy Hazarika were compiled from their published articles in various media formats which include online content as well.

Conclusion

In a concluding remark it can be said that:

1. Media commertialisation has lead to producers concentrate on market audience research programmes to design media texts which often results in homogeneity of products.
2. It was also confirmed that as stereotypical projection of late has been neglecting many other facets of reality, the role of media in specific reference to Northeast and Assam requires to be re-looked into for proper projection.
3. It is a concern today that if media disposes enough responsibility that comes with the immense power, to handle serious social issues, to take human emotion further to social development without hurting sentiments and not enraging people.
4. Points that emerge from interviews and gathered views
   " A majority of the respondents do show a serious concerns in the way Assam has been and is being represented in media in the state and as well as outside the state.
   " Commercialisation is a factor for which media content has been stereotypical.
   " The region only gets attention and due space in media when a large number of people are affected usually by violence or by flood.

- Geographical location makes the region out of reach and proximity area of the so called mainstream media organizations which makes authentication, validation, and understanding difficult along with negligence and lesser knowledge.
- There are norms which media houses need to follow regarding representation of violence in media, but is less maintained.
- The print media still has certain control on its content of violence, for direct depiction of violence usually images are selected over a span of time.
- In case of television media, there is no thumb rule for direct representation of violence. Most of the time acts of violence are telecasted under the 'LIVE' tag with no scope for selection or editing of footages.
- Other aspects of the region are never brought up in media.

Based on the responses obtained, it was reconfirmed that news from the region with the basic motive of information communication, is mostly a glimpse of the actual (people, places or events) most of which is either unknown or unexplored reality; and rest is not represented in media except the sensational part which is only understood as being capable of attracting a large spectrum of varied audience far and across. Out of the respondents of various strata of the media industry, academicians and locals the consensus was on the way Northeast has been projected outside the region through violence only.

The northeastern region suffers from certain discrimination from the mainstream media, and only selective events get exposed to the world, while other facets of life in the region are ignore by media. Only conflicts get reported and the resultant loss in life and property receive media exposure. This results in strong prejudice formation and reinforcement through stereotypical representations for long now. Thus it is seen that its need to be studied and applied in practice so as to confirm and see to it that the existing media bias is broken and perceptions changed.

It may be assumed that before the situation aggravates beyond control, the media in Northeast India and also the mainstream media, must take adequate steps to reduce violence in its content. And it is possible by expressing the concern that should not only be what is being projected but also on how it is being projected. The concentration has been on bringing the region to the headlines, and headlines are grabbed only with violence is the understanding. The real sharing of people's aspiration and the self motivation in to achieve shall reflect in controlling the frustration relevancies.

The above findings are on the effort of a research study being carried out in IIT Guwahati focusing on media reporting of violence specific to Assam and the Northeastern region in general. Work is still going on and is expected to generate means and methods through the locals aspirations that can be used for a positive imaging of the place and community in media overall benefit and development.

References

Baruah, Sanjib (2005), Durable Disorder: Understanding the Politics of Northeast India, Oxford University Press, New Delhi, p 61.

Baruah, Sanjib (1999), India Against Itself: Assam and the Politics of Nationality, University of Pennsylvania Press, Philadelphia.

Biswas, Prasenjit and C. Joshua Thomas (2006), Peace in India's North-East: Meaning, Metaphor, and Method : Essays of Concern and Commitment, Daya Books, New Delhi.

Chakrabarti Payel (2011a), Media and Health: Reference to Representations, Design and Content, 98th Indian Science Congress, Chennai, p 286.

Chakrabarti Payel and Das Liza (2012), Negative imaging of the Northeast India with reference to media marketisation, proc. National Seminar on Journalism in the Age of New Media, Surendranath College for Women, Kolkata, p 17.

Gupta, Om (2006), Encyclopaedia of Journalism and Mass Communication. Gyan Books, Delhi.

Hazarika, Sanjoy (1994), Strangers of the Mist: Tales of War and Peace from India's Northeast, Viking, New Delhi, p 63.

Kallarackal, Emmanuel Babu Joseph (2007), Peace Education in Northeast India: NESNIM as a Model of Peace Education in Multi-ethnic Settings, ProQuest, Ann Arbor, p 89.

Kamalipour, Yahya R and Kuldip R. Rampal.eds (2001), Media, Sex, Violence, and Drugs in the Global Village, Rowman & Littlefield, USA.

Kum?ra, Braja Bih?r? (2007), Problems of Ethnicity in the North-East India, Concept Publishing Company, New Delhi, p 44.

Singh, Jai Prakash eds. (1998), Trends in Social Sciences and Humanities in North East India, 1947-97. Daya Books, New Delhi, p 146-147.

Convergence of ICT/New Media Ethical Issues

Navpreet Kaur*

Globalization and digital convergence in the emerging knowledge society has raised complex ethical, legal and societal issues. We are facing more complications and difficulties regarding the freedom of expression, access to information, the right to privacy, intellectual property rights, and cultural diversity. ICT is an instrumental need of all humans for the gathering of information and knowledge, and as such, should be guaranteed as a basic right to all human beings. All over the world, rights that are already legally recognized are daily being violated, whether in the name of economic advancement, political stability, religious causes, the campaign against terrorism, or for personal greed and interests. Violations of these rights have created new problems in human social systems, such as the digital divide, cybercrime, digital security and privacy concerns, all of which have affected people's lives either directly or indirectly.

The study will focus on the growing issue of cyber crime. And on the other side the need of strong law and censorship. It is important that the government and society must come up with an assessment of the situation, followed by guidelines for action to combat the incidence of malicious attacks on the confidentiality,

Assistant Professor
Department of Journalism & Mass Communication
Guru Nanak Dev University, Regional Campus, Ladhewali, Jalandhar (Punjab)

integrity and availability of electronic data and systems, computer-related crimes, such as forgery and fraud, content related offenses, such as those related to child pornography, and violations of intellectual property rights (IPRs). Further, threats to critical infrastructure and national interests arising from the use of the internet for criminal and terrorist activities are of growing concern. The harm incurred to business houses, governments and individuals in those countries in which the internet is used widely, is gaining in scope and importance, while in other countries; cybercrime threatens the application of information and communication technology for government services, health care, trade, and banking.

As users start losing confidence in transactions and business, the opportunity costs may become substantial. The challenges reportedly, lie mainly in the general lack of awareness of information security issues, the rapidly evolving complexity of systems, the increasing capacity and reach of information and communication technology.

Cybercrime is a global problem that threatens all economies universally. As a crime that is committed across national borders, it requires cooperative, pro-active approaches in support of the less developed countries.

The objective of this paper is to compile:

i. Information concerning ethical issues in the country regarding:

i. Digital Divide
ii. Intellectual Property Rights
iii. Piracy
iv. Cybercrime
v. Human Rights

ii. Information on the initiatives and programmes undertaken at the local, national, regional, and international levels.

Introduction:

Information technology is impacting all walks of life all over the world. ICT developments have made possible a transition in information storage, processing, and dissemination, from paper to virtual and from atoms to bits, which are now setting new standards of speed, efficiency, and accuracy in human activities. Computerized databases are extensively used to store all sorts of confidential data of political, social, economic or personal nature to support human activities and bringing various benefits to the society.

However, the rapid development of ICT globally also has led to the growth of new forms of national and transnational crimes. These crimes have virtually no boundaries and may affect any country across the globe. Thus, there is a need for awareness, policy formation, and enactment of necessary legislation in all countries for the prevention of computer related crime. Globally, internet and computer-based commerce and communications cut across territorial boundaries thereby creating a new realm of human activities, and undermining the feasibility and legitimacy of applying laws based on geographic boundaries. The new boundaries, which are manifested in the monitor screens, firewalls, passwords, intruder detection, and virus busters, have created new personalities, groups, organizations, and other new forms of social, economic, and political groupings in the cyber world of bits. Traditional border-based law making and law enforcing authorities find this new environment of cyber boundaries very challenging.

Cyber systems across the globe have many different rules governing the behavior of users. Users are completely free to join or leave any system whose rules they find comfortable or uncomfortable. This flexibility may at times lead to improper user conduct. Also, in the absence of any suitable legal framework, it may be difficult for System Administrators to check on frauds, vandalism or other abuses, which may cause the lives of many online users to be miserable. This situation is alarming because any element of distrust for the internet may lead to people avoiding doing transactions online, thereby directly affecting the growth of e-commerce. The use or misuse of the internet as a medium of communication may in some situations lead to direct damage to real physical society. Non-imposition of taxes on online transactions may have its destructive effect on physical businesses, and also government revenues. Terrorists may also make use of the web to create conspiracies and violence. Wide and free sharing of ideologies, beliefs, convictions, and opinions between different cultures might cause physical and emotional stress and confusion that might lead to physical violence.

What is Ethics

In the last decade, dozens of ethics centres and programmes devoted to business ethics, legal ethics, bioethics, medical ethics, engineering ethics, and computer ethics have sprung up. These centres are designed to examine the implications of moral principles and practices in all spheres of human activity on our lives. Ethics can be viewed from two angles, normative and prescriptive. First, ethics refers to well-based standards of right and wrong that prescribe what humans ought to do, usually in terms of rights, obligations, benefits to society, fairness, and specific virtues. Ethics, for example, refers to those standards that impose the reasonable obligations to refrain from rape, stealing, murder, assault, slander, and fraud. Ethical standards also include those that enjoin virtues of honesty, compassion, and loyalty. And, ethical standards include standards relating to rights, such as the right to life, the right to freedom from injury, the right to choose, the right to privacy, and right to freedom of speech and expression. Such standards are adequate standards of ethics because they are supported by consistent and well-founded reasons.

Secondly, ethics refers to the study and development of personal ethical standards, as well as community ethics, in terms of behaviour, feelings, laws, and social habits and norms which can deviate from more universal ethical standards. So it is necessary to constantly examine one's standards to ensure that they are reasonable and well-founded. Ethics also means, then, the continuous effort of studying of our own moral beliefs and conduct, and striving to ensure that we, and our community and the institutions we help to shape, live up to standards that are reasonable and solidly-based for the progress of human beings.

Definition

"Ethics are moral standards that help guide behaviour, actions, and choices. Ethics are grounded in the notion of responsibility (as free moral agents, individuals, organizations, and societies are responsible for the actions that they take) and accountability (individuals, organizations, and society should be held accountable to others for the consequences of their actions). In most societies, a system of laws codifies the most significant ethical standards and provides a mechanism for holding people, organizations, and even governments accountable." (Laudon, et al, 1996)

ICT Ethics

ICT ethics are not exceptional from the above-mentioned view of ethics. In a world where information and communication technology has come to define how people live and work, and has critically affected culture and values, it is important for us to review ethical issues, as well as social responsibility, in the Asia-Pacific region. This is a difficult task because of the diversity in creed, class, caste, dialect, language, culture and race throughout the region. Moreover, the issue of ICT ethics takes on added significance as the region struggles with the dynamics of globalization and the current political environment after the September 11 incident.

ICT Ethical Issues

Analyzing and evaluating the impact of a new technology, such as ICT, can be very difficult. ICT does not only involve technological aspects, but also epistemology since the main component of ICT is information which represents data, information, and knowledge. ICT assists and extends the ability of mankind to capture, store, process, understand, use, create, and disseminate information at a speed and scale which had never been thought possible before. Some of the impact and changes of ICT are obvious, but many are subtle. Benefits and costs need to be studied closely for a nation to progress and improve the quality of life for its citizens. Issues that have arisen from the adoption of ICT, such as the application of automated teller machines (ATM), can be summarized as follows (Baase, 1997)

Unemployment

The automation of work has caused creative destruction by eliminating some vocations and creating new ones. How does this affect the employment or unemployment of the work force of a nation?

Crime

Stolen and counterfeit ATM cards are used to steal millions of dollars each year throughout the region. The anonymity of the machines makes some crimes easier and creates many new types of crimes.

Loss of privacy

Transactions are transmitted and recorded in databases at banks, hospitals, shopping complexes, and various organizations, in the public or private sector. The contents of electronic communications and databases can provide important and private information to unauthorized individuals and organizations if they are not securely guarded.

Errors

Information input into the databases is prone to human and device error. Computer programmes that process the information may contain thousands of errors. These errors can create wrong and misleading information about individuals and organizations. Information and programme errors might result in financial loss, or even the loss of lives.

Intellectual property

Millions of dollars of software is illegally copied each year all over the world. This phenomenon has a great impact on the software industry in the region. Local and foreign software industries need consumers support all over the world to maintain the progress of technology. Most importantly, for the sake of growth in indigenous ICT innovation and invention, local software industries in Asia-Pacific need local support in protecting their intellectual property rights and investment.

Freedom of speech and press

How do the constitutional rights of individuals in terms of the freedoms of speech and press apply to electronic media? How seriously do the problems of pornography, harassment, libel, and censorship on the net affect individuals and society? What government initiatives have been used in handling this crisis?

Digital Divide

How does ICT affect local community life? The increasing use of computers has increased the separation of rich and poor, creating a digital divide between the information "haves" and "have-nots." What subsidies and programmes have been provided by governments of the region to address the issue?

Professional Ethics

How well trained and ethical are our ICT professionals in dispensing their duties? Faulty and useless systems that cause disasters and hardships to users might be built by incompetent ICT professionals. In dispensing their duties ICT professionals must demonstrate their best practices and standards as set by professional bodies for quality assurance.

UNESCO's Info-Ethics Programme

The development of digital technologies and their application in worldwide information networks are opening vast new opportunities for efficient access to and use of information by all societies. All nations can fully benefit from these opportunities on the condition that they meet the challenges posed by these information and communication technologies. Thus, UNESCO's Info-Ethics Programme was established for the principal objective of reaffirming the importance of universal access to information in the public domain, and to define ways that this can be achieved and maintained in the Global Information Infrastructure. It seeks to address the areas of ethical, legal and societal challenges of cyberspace, as well as privacy and security concerns in cyberspace. It aims to encourage international cooperation in the following aspects: (http://www.unesco.org/webworld/public_domain/legal.html)

- ¢ Promotion of the principles of equality, justice and mutual respect in the emerging Information Society;
- ¢ Identification of major ethical issues in the production, access, dissemination, preservation and use of information in the electronic environment; and
- ¢ Provision of assistance to Member States in the formulation of strategies and policies on these issues.

Ethical issues Derived from New Technology

Technological advances present numerous advantages, provided the right infrastructure is put in place to allow organizations to make the best possible use of relevant opportunities. In emerging economies, knowledge presents a key competitive advantage to organizations and people. There is a need, therefore, to formulate a clear vision than would give way to appropriate values, skills and professional competencies required of intelligent and knowledge-based systems. New approaches to leadership, human resource development, organizational development/change management, and information and communication technologies should be developed. Information must be managed differently because information flows take the form of communicated knowledge of a comprehensive nature. Knowledge-based systems have developed rapidly in both the Western world and in major industrialized nations like China and India. Along with this growing importance of information and communication technologies (ICTs) however, numerous ethical issues have emerged. While ICTs have become omnipresent in contemporary life, we cannot oversee the ethical problems that are experienced as such technologies evolve. These issues include access to ICT infrastructure and education; distribution and use of power; corrupt practices in the form of bribery and favouritism; infringement of property rights and/or property theft; information gathering through spying. Following this, the question arises whether 'new ethics' is needed to handle ethical issues arising from technological advances.

While Mehra et al. (2004) lay emphasis on the "potential of the Internet to improve everyday life for those on the margins of society and to achieve greater social equity and empowerment" (p. 782), numerous scholars, policy makers and the public at large have expressed concern over the negative impact of technological advances. Although there is the logical expectation that globalisation should impact positively on any nation, ethical issues arising with the advent of knowledge-based systems should not be underestimated. Of the main forces that lead to ethical problems in emerging knowledge-based economies are technology, globalization, and access to education. As technology revolutionizes the nature and speed of communication across nations, the risks that accompany such rapid evolution - cyber crimes; hacking; cyber scams and frauds; Internet defamation; software piracy; copyright infringement - cannot be overlooked. In the business community, the Internet is considered as a major channel for commercial transactions. Consequently, on-line business has given rise to several potential ethical issues relating to honesty and integrity; responsibility, accountability, privacy and confidentiality, protection of data (e.g. credit card numbers), freedom from invasiveness (e.g. websites that automatically track and retain customer contact and information). Other issues at stake include the quality of goods delivered, disclosure and reliability of information, sources of goods, and Internet economics versus traditional economics. Internet economics compels us to consider the impacts of global Internet business, employment through the net (e.g. local and global telecommuting), web advertising, competition on the Internet (computer hacking and falsification of data), and public information and financial disclosure. Technological evolution is inevitably going to lead to disparities across borders, hence the significance of the digital divide.

Likely Outcome of The Digital Divide

'Digital divide/gap' refers to the disparity between those populations who have regular, effective access to digital and information technology and those without equivalent access. It generally encompasses both physical access to technology hardware and more broadly, skills and resources and that allow for its use. It can refer to both international as well as domestic disparities in access to information technology. It can also refer to the skills people have - the divide between people who are at ease using technology to access and to analyze information and those who are not.

More expansively, the digital divide is referred to as "a symptom of a larger and more complex problem: the problem of persistent poverty and inequality" (Servon, 2002: 2). Mehra et al. (2004) lay emphasis on the four major components that contribute to digital divide. These are "socioeconomic status, with income, educational level and race among other factors associated with technological attainment" (p. 782). The digital divide could be the outcome of various factors worldwide. There are certain measures that can be adopted if the aim is to improve business relations across frontiers.

Forces like communication technology, modern infrastructure and free trade enable greater mobility for people, thereby facilitating interaction amongst business partners (Hagan and Moon, 2006). Technological advances are bound to differ across countries, and the digital divide is bound to have more serious repercussions on emerging knowledge-based economies that have limited means to invest in information and communication technology. In such an environment, business people are more likely to engage in questionable practices in an effort to either 'match' the standard of their business counterparts on the global market, or simply avail of 'opportunities' that lead to easy money. The digital divide could also be the outcome of an imbalance of diffusion of ICT infrastructure, high online charges, insufficiently trained staff, and imperfect network legation and information resource shortage in international languages. Some less wealthy nations may have difficulty achieving connectivity, in particular in rural areas. The lack of purchasing power or low population densities in less favourable regions could deter telecommunication providers from investing in broadening their networks.

Inevitably income constitutes a problem in emerging knowledge-based systems. Even if the problem of infrastructure for connectivity is resolved in suburbs, high costs of Internet-compatible computers still have to be faced. Market forces may push Internet Service Providers to "shy away from investing in these regions that show little promise of short-term profits" (Wilhelm, 2004: 133-134).

Wilhelm's findings imply that preference is given to more favourable areas, more than likely urban settings to the detriment of rural ones, in some countries. Education levels can potentially influence computer access and access to the Internet: those with higher levels of education are more likely to be equipped with information and communication technologies. Similarly, education is closely correlated to income, which obviously facilitates the purchase of ICTs and inclusion in both home and work settings. However, when income levels are taken into account, those with higher educational achievements may benefit of higher rates of access. It is equally important to note that disparities in education levels are a reality in the developing world.

Abuse of Position and Ethical Transgression

Illiteracy constitutes a major problem in emerging economies, where knowledge-based systems have yet to be consolidated. In some places, public expenditure is manipulated and driven away from growth-promoting areas and essential services like education and ICTs. Sometimes public funds are diverted to where bribes are easy to collect. The culture of corruption that prevails in developing nations diverts public goods from ever reaching the poor. In addition, the latter are victimized as they are expected to pay bribes for public services that they are entitled to, free of- charge (Werhane et al., 2008). There are even instances where the authorities hold back their services because they have no guarantee of economic payoff. Already there is evidence of a concentration of public spending in low productivity projects such as large-scale construction to the detriment of value-enhancing investments like improvements in the quality of social infrastructure and ICTs (Blackburn et al., 2006).

The abuse of discretionary power and monopolistic nature of the State can only breed ethical issues by increasing the inequity between rich and poor countries. In countries with an individualistic culture where the concept of particularism prevails, there is the perception that one's immediate obligation goes to one's relations. This view overrides one's notion of duty as spelled out by basic concepts of ethics. This can in turn give rise to corrupt practices in the form of favouritism and nepotism.

Democracy in emerging economies tends to encourage the abuse of power to suit one's vested interests. These nations may not have effective systems of checks and balances, which tends to give way to greater political access coupled with greater flexibility with the way public funds are dispensed (Mohtadi and Roe, 2001). The abuse or misuse of funds directly impacts on the progress of an economy. Emerging knowledge-based systems tend to be at a disadvantage if the political class uses their discretionary power, giving priority to low-productivity projects to the detriment of vital services like education and ICTs, which are prerequisites to the proper development of knowledge, based systems.

Traditionally, intellectual property belonged to developed countries. Therefore, the developed world regards the protection of intellectual property as important, given that such property brings wealth to mankind and helps achieve progress. However, developing countries have cultural achievements such as their cultural heritage and folk arts that they consider valuable and thus, deserve to be protected as well. Intellectual property may be tangible or intangible. Are intangible forms of property like software, product formulation, formulae, inventions or processing techniques recognized as such? Intangible property can be far more valuable and difficult to protect than tangible assets. It is hard to put a value on intangible assets like the ability to innovate; codified knowledge about products and processes; employee assets in the form of talented people and human capital. While being highly precious to the organization, these assets are also vulnerable to infringement and theft (Hagan and Moon, 2006).

Property theft can take the form of insider trading, counterfeit products, or price gouging. Insider trading takes place when one uses privileged information as one's own. A common form of theft is the use of proprietary information to further another firm's ends. Such information is normally accessed through the unauthorized use of company computers and programmes (Fritzsche, 2005). What exactly constitutes ethical transgression? What restrictions can and should be placed on different forms of property, including digital information? If people in poor countries feel that they are not at par with their business partners on the global market, they could engage in unethical competitive behaviour in an attempt to match the performance of their rivals. Crane and Matten (2004) refer to industrial espionage through questionable practices in the normal business settings in European context. Business people can instigate a process of intelligence gathering through spying by having recourse to suspicious means. In the process, the legal and ethical practices underlying conventional information gathering or market research are deliberately flouted. Spying and information gathering can potentially contravene the privacy and confidentiality of competitors and/or other stakeholders. In places where bribery represents a normal way of doing business, illicit payments can be offered to induce competitors' employees to access confidential information and trade secrets.

If all these issues are taken into consideration, it is obvious that knowledge-based systems are at risk. In order to protect themselves and to retain their goodwill, business people may have to invest in resources to preserve trade secrets, patents, copyrights, trademarks and intellectual property rights including rights on intangible property like software, product formulation, processing techniques, to name but a few. The development of new technologies will keep encouraging ethical debates on what exactly constitutes intellectual property (Crane and Matten, 2004; Ghillyer, 2008). Taking all this into account, there is a need to acknowledge the seriousness of problems that can potentially be caused by forces driving change in global context. The next part of our discussion focuses on whether we need new ethics to address the ethical issues accompanying technological progress.

On the other side, Human Rights Protection in Cyberspace is an extension of traditional Human Rights that are available in a real life situation. With the growing use of Information and Communication Technology (ICT) in our day to day affairs, our Human Rights in Cyberspace are frequently violated by Governmental as well as Non-Governmental entities, persons and organizations. The traditional "Welfare States" are now working as "E-Police States" and "Endemic E-Surveillance States". The ICT Trends In India 2009 clearly established this position in India.

Civil Liberties like Privacy Rights, Right to Speech and Expression, Right to Data Protection, Right against E-Surveillance by State, Right against Internet Censorship by State, Right to Information, etc are in serious jeopardy due to growing and unaccounted governmental intrusions and violations.

To safeguard our Human Rights in Cyberspace we need an effective Techno-Legal Framework. At the same time we also need "Private Defense in Cyberspace" against an overzealous and over guarded E-Police State.

This initiative would act as a "Centre for Protection of Human Rights in Cyberspace" and aims at providing techno-legal framework as well as means and tools to exercise private defense in cyberspace against Governmental and Non Governmental violators and aggressors who violate Human Rights in Cyberspace without "Proper Authority" and "Constitutional Authority".

At the same time we would also provide a "Techno-Legal Framework" for Data Protection Law. In India, Privacy Rights Protection In India, formulation of Privacy Laws In India, Legal Frameworks for E-Governance in India, Legal Frameworks for E-Commerce in India, Legal Framework for implementation of Projects like Crime and Criminal Tracking Network & Systems (CCTNS) Project (CCTNS Project), National Intelligence Grid (NATGRID), Unique Identification Authority of India (UIDAI), National Counter

Terrorism Centre (NCTC) of India, E-Surveillance under the Information Technology Act 2000 (IT Act 2000) and other laws, etc.

Do We Need New Ethics?

Phenomena like illicit information gathering, unauthorized accessing and exploitation of intellectual property, property theft have accompanied on-going developments in technology (Crane and Matten, 2004). As computer ethics and digital divide continue to grow in importance globally, questions arise as to whether business ethics should be re-thought (Ghillyer, 2008; Hagan and Moon, 2006; Hartman and Desjardins, 2008; Suresh and Raghavan, 2005). Bearing in mind the characteristics of business, both the legislation and notions of ethics need to be reinforced to cope with changing tendencies as well as to handle the basic ethical issues that accompany new technology. Unless business people thoroughly understand the law, it will be hard to manage the ethical issues brought about by the misuse of communication technology. Alongside with the law, a culture of ethics should be instilled, so as to deter harmful business practices that can potentially lead to serious losses and long-term economic decline.

Ghillyer (2008) lays emphasis on the ten commandments of computer ethics and raises the question as to whether some new code should be adopted for the global community. In spite of the existence of the United Nations' Non Governmental Global Compact and the Organization for Economic Cooperation and Development Guidelines for Multinational Enterprises, ethical misconduct still exists in international business. Ghillyer (2008) proposes a global code of conduct as the solution to moral issues encountered in the context of globalization. Does the problem not lie with the interpretation of concepts of ethics and codes of ethics that is, with enforcement? After all, ethics codes exist worldwide but are subject to varying interpretation, as are universal principles. As they are not legally binding, codes of ethics tend to be regarded as optional while business people have a tendency to underestimate their importance, giving priority to short-term gains. While business partners should fulfill their responsibility towards their stakeholders, it is the duty of every responsible government to lead by example and breed a culture of ethics at national level. It is equally their responsibility to bridge the gap between rich and poor economies, and foster corporate social responsibility. They should sustain their efforts towards the convergence of ethics by providing the necessary infrastructure at national level. This includes putting in place appropriate telecommunication devices. There is evidence that political people, in emerging nations, sometimes welcome corporate investors under 'flexible' terms in an attempt to boost economic growth (Alatas, 1999). In this endeavour, public funds could easily be channeled towards sub-quality products, and intangible property in the area of ICTs constitutes no exception. If this were the case, governments could be deliberately inflicting economic and human rights abuses on their people in the name of growth. Alternatively, it can be argued that such behaviour suppresses the development of knowledge-based systems. Bearing all this in mind, ethics is there and should not only be viewed as an academic discipline. While there is no need for new ethics, both private and public sectors should reflect on their mode of doing business and ensure that they fulfill their duty towards their stakeholders. Technology offers a unique opportunity to extend learning support beyond the classroom, something unknown to the business community until recently. "The variety of functions that the Internet can serve for the individual user makes it 'unprecedentedly malleable' to the user's current needs and purposes" (Bargh and McKenna, 2004: 577). In addition to this view, there is a perception that the building of an information society is the key to economic development and modernization (Dey, 2005), implying that this would naturally pull an economy out of poverty. Ideally, new technology should contribute to the development of depressed regions and promote global citizenship and human rights amongst other positive things (Argandona, 2008; Richter and Mar, 2004). However, in economies or contexts where people do not understand technological improvement, they may not be as effectively positioned to benefit as quickly from such advances (Hartman and Desjardins, 2008). This implies that they may not be adequately prepared to handle the challenges associated with high-tech advancement. In the circumstances, the priority of major stakeholders - the government, state-owned enterprises, business entities, research institutes, and universities - should be to invest in the right infrastructure so as to educate their people. Governments should invest in education and continuous learning, so as to ensure that every citizen benefits from equal chances.

Telecommunications infrastructure should be developed and sustained in a consistent manner with proper strategies thinking. Should governments of emerging nations not pursue reform as part of their national policy to promote their economy on the global market through science and technology? Should they not encourage industrialization by virtue of IT development and explore means of further developing information technology to accommodate their own needs on economic, social and political fronts? Does the fact that the domestic telecommunication market is gradually opening up to foreign investors and competitors not justify increasing investment in the telecommunication arena, in emerging knowledge-based systems? Countries that are members of international bodies like the World Trade Organization are at an advantage. Such affiliation acts as an external drive force for them to persevere at pursuing and sustaining reform in the field of telecommunications and technology. Technological reform should be the priority of all economies involved in global operations, irrespective of how developed they are.

Information strategies and policies should support and enable a knowledge culture. At a national level, we need proper legislative, regulatory and fiscal frameworks that encourage and support the creation and sharing of knowledge, thereby enhancing creativity and innovation. Educational institutions and Governments should establish appropriate information literacy skills and behaviours that the education system and lifelong learning programmes must provide, for the smooth evolution of the knowledge based system. Both organizational and individual competitiveness should be promoted in emerging knowledge settings. Government policy should make provision for the development and promotion of standards and good practices that would help manage all types of information in knowledge-based organizations, while easing organizational competitiveness. At an individual level, new skills and behaviours should be encouraged to enable individuals optimize their potential and play an active role in the evolution of the knowledge-based system.

Along with organizational and individual competitiveness, information profession competitiveness - through embracing, informing and stimulating the wider information profession on all issues relating to the management of information in the knowledge-based system - should be enhanced. Governments that do not respond to the challenges and opportunities presented by the emerging knowledge based system would face the risk of their economy becoming increasingly marginalized on the global market, as competitors take up emerging challenges and opportunities.

Conclusion

There is no single approach to using ICT for development purposes. Most countries have a national policy on ICT in place. What is lacking is a comprehensive framework on how to use ICT to meet the needs of the poor, vulnerable and marginalized groups. Countries need a specific policy or action plan to realize the potential benefits of ICT, foster sustainable development, empower people, including women and youth, build capacity and skills, assist small and medium-sized enterprises and reinforce popular participation in decision-making at all levels. Attention should also be given to the issues of cultural and linguistic diversity, the ethical dimensions of ICT usage, the use of the right technology (which is cost-effective and user-friendly) and human resources development.

In addition to framing sound ICT policy, Governments need the political will to implement it. Before ICT can work for the poor, Governments first need to create an enabling environment by preparing innovative policies for the sector, strengthening institutions and improving infrastructure and connectivity. Distance education cannot function without a school with electricity; telemedicine will not work if hospitals do not exist. Second, Governments need to concentrate on "application programmes" to enable understanding of the development linkages among various sectors. Governments should involve ICT service providers and agencies working in poverty alleviation in developing the institutional mechanisms of ICT policy. Third, they need to improve ICT awareness, develop skills and human resources to create sufficient demand and manage the sector properly. Attention should also be given to monitoring the impact of ICT projects and adjusting projects on the basis of experience.

Referring to the ethical issues likely to result from new technologies in a global era - access to ICT infrastructure and education; distribution and use of power; infringement of property rights; information gathering through spying - contemporary ethicists raise the question as to whether 'new ethics' is needed.

References

1. Argandona, A., 'The New Economy: Ethical Issues', Journal of Business Ethics vol. 20, 2008, pp. 3-22.
2. Bargh, J. A., & McKenna, K. Y. A., 'The Internet and Social Life', Annual Review of Psychology vol. 55, 2004, pp. 573-590.

3. Blackburn, K., Bose, N., & Haque, M. E., 'The Incidence and Persistence of Corruption in Economic Development', The Journal of Economic Dynamics and Control, vol. 30, 2006, pp. 2447-2467.

4. Crane, A., & Matten, D., Business Ethics: a European Perspective, New York: Oxford University Press, 2004.

5. Dey, B. R., Business Process Engineering and Change Management, Bizantra: Innovations in Management, 2005.

6. Fritzsche, D. J., Business Ethics: a Global and Managerial Perspective, New York: McGraw Hill International Edition, 2005.

7. Ghillyer A. Business Ethics: a Real World Approach, New York: McGraw Hill, Irwin, 2008.

8. Hagan, J., & Moon, C. 'New Economy, New Ethics' in Business Ethics: Facing Up to the Issues, The Economist Books, London: Profile Books Ltd, 2006, pp. 7-21.

9. Hartman, L., & Desjardins, J., Business Ethics: Decision Making for Personal Integrity and Social Responsibility, New York: McGraw Hill International Edition, 2008.

10. Mehra, B.; Merkel, C, & Bishop, A. P., 'The Internet for Empowerment of Minority and Marginalised Users', New Media and Society, vol. 6, 2004, pp. 781-802.

11. Mohtadi, H., & Roe, T. L. 'Democracy, Rent Seeking, Public Spending and Growth', Journal of Public Economics, vol. 87, 2003, pp. 445-466.

12. Richter, F-J., & Mar, P. C. M.. Asia's New Crisis: Renewal through Total Ethical Management, World Economic Forum, Singapore: Wiley and Sons (Asia) Pte. Ltd, 2004.

13. Servon, L., Bridging the Digital Divide: Technology, Community and Public Policy, Malden, MA: Blackwell, 2002.

14. Suresh, J., & Raghavan, B. S. Professional Ethics, New Delhi: Chand & Co. Ltd, 2005.

15. Werhane, P., Kelley, S., Hartman, L., & Moberg, D., "Alleviating Poverty through Profitable Partnerships: Globalisation, Markets and Economic Well-Being", Unpublished Manuscript, (2008).

16. Wilhelm, A. G., Digital Nation: Towards an Inclusive Information Society, Cambridge, MA: MIT Press, 2004.

Comment by Sarvesh Dutt Tripathi

Only foreign perspective while it has become a major issue in our country where use of cybermedia is growing very fast? No mention of Pawan Duggal, an Indian who is known for cybermedia ethics and laws in India. Anyway well explained the issue.

Development and Media: Rhetoric and Reality

Dr. Dharmendra Singh

After the Second World War, the whole world had divided into two parts; capitalist and socialist blocks. America represented capitalism while Soviet Russia represented socialism. Their goals were different. One wanted the media should not be regulated by the state; it should have freedom and the free flow of information. The other had a socialistic point of view; it thought that media should not be free it should be under the control of the state. Thus America believed in the free flow of the information and liberal, free market discourse that championed the rights of media proprietors to sale whatever and wherever they wished. They believe that though the development of the world is possible through the free flow of the information. America thought the international communication was the key to the process of modernization and development for the third world. America gave birth to the concept of developmental media theory and international mass communication theory which could be used to spread the message of modernity. This would result in the transfer of the economic and the political model of the west to the newly independent countries of the south. The developmental theory firmly believes that it can remove traditional thinking in order to make the people equal on the basis of socio economic, political cultural, educational, psychological equality of opportunities.

Deniel Lerner, who was professor of political science at the Massachusetts Institute of Technology, was the exponent of this theory. His classical work in this field is The Passing of Traditional Society; Modernizing the Middle East (1958) in which he proposed that contact with the media helped the process of transition from a traditional to a modernized state. He characterized the mass media as a mobility multiplier which enables individuals to experience events in for-off- places, forcing them to reassess their traditional way of life. Exposure to the media Learner argued made traditional society less bound by traditions and made them aspire to a new and modern way of life. He thinks that the west's developmental path which improves the living conditions of societies is useful. It can remove the backwardness of the rest of the nations. His belief was that the western society had the most developed model of societal attributes (power, wealth, skills; rationality) and with the help of these thing; imbalance of the world mostly in the underdeveloped countries could be removed.

Learner's social development model consisted of the following components (S.R. Melkote and H.L. Steeves' communication for development in the third world page 114)

a. A core of mobile individuals whose psychological orientation made it easier to accept rapid changes in their personal lives and the overall social system.

b. An omnipotent mass media system that reinforced and accelerated societal and individual change by the disseminating the new ideas and thoughts and attitudes conducive to modernization, and

c. The corelation between the Important indices of urbanization literacy, media exposure and economic and political participation to establish a modern western type society.

Those countries which were colony of developed (North) countries till second world war, after it became indepent state, their socio economic conditions were measarable and this was not threating to its own rich people but also the rich of the rich countries (developed). That is why in 1949 US President Truemen made point four programme for the people of the third world countries which is the US would support the UN and help strengthen its ability to enforce its decisions. Second, the US would continue its work in revitalizing the world economy. Third, the US would "strengthen freedom-saving peoples around the world against the evil of aggression. Fourth, The US would embark on a new programme of modernization and capital investment".

Deniel Lerner, Wilbur Sehramm, Rogers and some others are motivated by the policy of Truman and moved toward the path of A.H. Maslow's which is known as Self-Actualization (A sense of self-fulfillment, deeper meaning in life's accomplishments; a sense of "happiness") which comes after the essential physiological requirement of food and shelter, the foundation of physical survival. Once those needs are met, concern of the second level can be considering the need for safety and security from the external threats. When the needs of first and second level are met, only then does Maslow see the human being as focusing on the happiness factors such as developing friendships, love relationships, and building up a sense of affiliation by being concern with social interaction. At that point the individual becomes concerned with self-esteem and gaining esteem from others. And finally, the self-actualization where, with the previous levels needs satisfied, a person experiences a need to reach full potential through maximum use of skill and abilities. This is A.H. Maslow's development (happiness, self-actualization). And all the modernization communications theorists directly or indirectly want to get it.

Another staunch follower of this theory is Wilbur Schramm. His well popular book is entitled Mass Media and National Development published in 1964 in which he prepared that mass media serves as a bridge to a wider world, a vehicle for transforming new ideas and models from the north (Developed) to the south (Underdeveloped, Developing) and within the south from urban to rural areas. But he feels that this one is not easy task as he says —"It takes a long time to modernize traditional agriculture not so much because the task is expensive as because it requires teaching new skills and new attitude and persuading cultivators to give up ancient practices and strongly held belief providing modern transportation, communication power and other social overhead tasks along time because it is very costly and requires a number of highly skilled worker and manager who are in short supply and must be trained. Education is slow not only because it is costly to train and pay techer bad build schools but also because education is by nature a slow process."

And he again says :

> "Where modern communication becomes so important to economic development. For the task of the mass media of information and the new media of education is to speed and ease the long, slow social transformation required for economic development and in particular to speed and smooth the task of mobilizing human resources behind the national effort."

It was the impact of the Schramm's book upon the United Nation which made them proclaims 1960's as the decade of development. In 1970 all the theorists of this field started this war for the development of society. The new approach was top-down approach to communications, a one way flow of information from the authority or the western developed agencies (with the help of mass media) to the southern, underdeveloped countries, without any feedback. They never asked whom they wanted to modernize and in what way. They also kept silent as to who would gain or lose. They denied any dimensions of development. In many southern countries, the income disparities increased over the succeeding forty years despite a growth in GNP.

We should not, however, forget that this development media theory has already improved the condition of the people a lot. The change of this theory creating local 'elites' is unfounded since there is no such intention implicit. It is another matter through those local elites does not want other to be equal to them. They had centered all the resources and did not go to disseminate. Thus, people in the underdeveloped countries think that earlier they were colonized by the west, now they have been colonized by their own race, casts and community's elites. Galtuing's is theary of Structural Imperialism in which the whole sociaty is divided two part core and periphery where core is so powerful which does not want that plriphery should come at that level where it is. This structure can he seen at every level, status strata of Indian sociaty.

Those people who have been repressed for centuries should not ask for their rights even the most primary once and that the other backward classes should not ask for reservations because it will infiltrate into those reservation if Brahmin and Kshatriya which have been in practices for centuries though without written character. Now it is clear to all that the trinity-politician, capitalists and media persons are united and always try to distribute the benefits of the society among them. They can be come close to be phrase of Parson and Paroto 'Circulation of Eletes. Politicians make rules which help capitalists and capitalists run media houses which helps politician to spread their vested interest content among the masses which helps the politicians to maintain their status quo.

Honourable V.P. Singh's Government passed Mandal Commission in 1990 to improve the living condition of poor section of Indian society which was very negatively presented by the Brahmin-Baniya oriented Indian media. What is highly understandable in this whole episode is the media has been able to create impressions that the posts filled through reservation are posts filled by incompatible people and posts filled without reservation are filled with competent people, the unwritten reservation notwithstanding. As analysis of requirements in center and states universities will show that the academic criteria has been the list consideration where as castes and another political factors have got a candidate selected.

The following practically example of central university will show the level of partiality and the violations of norms in practices, B.H.U. data, Banaras Hindu University Varanasi, Uttar Pradesh.

The media reports that reservation has been in practice for too long and the government should cancel now. The truth is that reservation posts have never been filled to their fault capacity, partly because of political reasons and practically the candidates are not available. A cursory glance at the overall of posts vacant in Indian universities. Otherwise mend for ST/SC and OBC, will make the position clear, lecturer in the department, on the cost of Dr. Jai Krishna, an internationally reputed scholar in geology. Academic achievement of Jai Krishna and M, Joshi is given below on other candidates V.K. Gairola's detail is also put here for comparison.

In this connection, it deserve mentioning that V.K. Gairola, at that time Head, was not only a known bootlicker of the V.C. but also a relative of M. Joshi through Murli Manohar Joshi the former H.R.D. Minsiter of N.D.A. (BJP Leader), The maternal uncle of the latter.

Bio-data of J. Krishna Vs M. Joshi & V. K Gairola

1. Number of Research Papers

a.	International	55	07	05
b.	National	45	14	15

2. Cititation abroad abundant Rare None

3. Teaching experiences

a.	PG	25 Years	30	05
b.	UG	28	30	12

4. Independent Ph.D. Supervision

03	06	None

5. Fellowship & assignments abroad

15	00	00

6. Chairmanship conferences

a.	International	02	None	None
b.	National	01	None	None

7. Invited Lectures abroad

25	None	None

8. Membership of International Bodies

10	None	None

9. Research Projects

a.	International	05	None	None
b.	National	05	None	02

Near about 35 pages detail are given by Dr. Subhash Rai in his book Clique formation and academic deterioration in Indian University (A case study of the Banaras Hindu University in 1998 which was publihsed by Radha Krishna publication Varanasi), B.H.U. where the picture of nepotism and castism could be seen which is indirectly exploiting the rights of others (Orientalist).

These orientlist or third world people's condition is prtray in the Myth of Development by O.De Rivero (2001) Page 63-64,

> "The country formerly known as the third world were always too politically, economically and culturally hetrogeneous to join forces as a world front based on common interest. Now, their interest are still more diverse and distant as the result of a greater differentiations in the levels of national misery among them. Divided into different groups, with greater of less poverty, the majority of this countries have not begun to compete in the prosperity rankings with the old aristocracy

of industrialized countries. Instead they continue to compete among themselves for the world poverty ratings. This situation is major obstacle for true economic globlization. Since it prevents the majority of the world's populations from becoming consumers of products from the transnational enterprises. For the devotees of Adam Smith's The Wealth of Nations, ironically, the concern today seems to be the poverty of nations."

World's near about twenty developing countries population earn less than one dollar a day, means under poverty. Whereas India is concerned its eighty percent population earn twenty Rs. Per day which is disclosed by Arjun Sen Gupta committee's report which was set up by the government of India. One thing should be clear here if this much population is in this miserable position then this is not their own fault but the fault of the rulers of them who are governed by the mind-set of aristocracy. Who decides world wide where, what, how, and for whom to produce what. As it is written by Oswaldo De Rivero in his classic book The Myth of Development page no. 46 that- :

"Today the destiny of many national economies and cultures is being decided not in government offices or parliaments but in Internation financial markets of New York, Chicago, London, Singapore, Hongkong, Tokyo, Frankfurt or Paris, and in the board-rooms of the transnational corporations."

Development means neither Europeanizatton nor Westernization (Husserl) nor Brahminization/Sanskritization (M.N Srinivas). It is an on going process which can only have work at its centre for the peace and prosperity of all. One develops with in as well as without. The view of Gandhi was that development should begin from the grass root level of society. He wanted every individual to share the power that in turn helps people govern society.

Whereas media is concerned, since its origin it is doing its own jobs which is guided and decided by the gate keepers (Kurt Lewin) and the dream of Mcluhan's Global village is turn into reality. But whereas a benefit to it is concerned till date only chosen few are benefited and maximum are deprived.

From the first to the fourth five-year plans, the situation of development was quantitatively improving but qualitatively, the position of downtrodden was more or less static as it were. It was in 1970 that the scene of authoritarianism was changed to some extent. The demand for freedom and for selection led to the awareness of right and duties in the minds of the people. All spheres of society were going to be aware of the way development was to take place. It was the key role of modern media, which was improving the status of the people. People, (with the help of radio and newspapers) got adequate information, which was utilized for improving the lives of India. Women's education child education, eradication of poverty became prime agenda. Emphasis upon the use of technique in agricultural farming led to higher growth rate. Other programme about health, poverty, and unemployment were disseminated by the radio and newspapers alike.

But the whole mass media of India was being regulated with western theories of development. The theories were unfamiliar about the Indian landscape reality and the problems, people in India faced. However, western theories did much and were not mere utopia. The dominant culture of the west was followed by the upper castes of India. The development problems are everywhere the same. The difference is inequality. The Soviet Union Theory held good in Europe, even in India. The demand to break the monopoly of power groups is essential for change. The demand of Indian people to disseminate real picture of events and fulfillments of common minimum needs to more or less the same things as the surplus theory of the Marx, which implied distribution to the needy.

We see that among the people of India, there is a general awareness to participate in power. The monopoly groups, however allow this. The majority in India has been marginalized for long. India is known as a democratic country where every individual in supposed to get equal opportunities in education, employment etc.

There is a need for theory, which could change the ideology of the old periods. Indians need to approach a more humans approach without division and limitations. The concept of 'Brotherhood' is urgently requirement at present. There has always been difference between theory and practice more so in. India, which bounds in destination. Indians are divided by race, caste, community, religious fanaticism, feelings of the upper and the lower which are not bringing equality among segments of Indian society. We still need a theory, which could remove all these inequalities thereby silencing violence revenge etc. The literary play theory could do so. Play implies a negative capability to enter into others and understand their feelings, needs, emotions etc. This will instill kindness, pity for the poor. The innovation, which the law cannot bring, will then be brought. People will know that there is no difference between the character they lived for the time being and they themselves. When this will come in the time come in the field of communication, only then the goals and objectives will be achieved. We can explain the play with the help of the friends between Krishna and Sudama. Krishna rules over a Kingdom while Sudama is a downtrodden. The king Krishna asks Sudama to sit on his own thrown without any feeling of status. The paradigm should serve to bring equality in society. Another example, from Ramcharit Manas is when Lord Ram eats the fruits given by Sebery, a tribal woman. Rama is not status conscious there, there are so many other such instances in our religious texts, we need a will power to change over society on the basis of such paradigms. Lord Buddha's acceptance of Pali rather than Sanskrit reveals that one should transfer one's thoughts into the mass language. Sanskrit was the language of the haves while Pali was spoken by the have nots. Budha, without any complaint, accepted Pali because he knew the pain of the common people who were not allowed participation in the mainstream culture or power structure.

लोहे का स्वाद
उस लौहार से मत पूछो
बल्कि, उस घोड़े से पूछो
जिसके मुंह में लगाम है।

धुमिल

Bibliography

Ambedkar, B.R. Ghandhian; The Doom of the Untouchable, in Fred Dollmayr And G. N. Devy(eds) Between Tradition and Modernity, New Delhi; Sage Publication 1998.

Berelson, B. and Janowitz, M.: Social Control In News Room. In Wilbur Schramm(ed.) Mass Communication University of Illinois Press,1960

Carr,E.H.: The New Society, London:Mac Millan, 1951

Derrida,J.:Grammatology Motilal Banarasidass Publishers, Delhi 1994

Empowering Women and Social Transformation

Shweta Chaturvedi* and Shreya Chakrabarty**

Abstract

Women's empowerment and social transformation has been an old endeavor towards larger and sustainable social development. Transformation may however, have different interpretations. It is important to question what "*power*" and "*transformation*" are and what they ought to be in relation to man-woman-societal dynamics? It can be viewed with a change in the thought processes of men that women are equally competent and not to be mocked at for their output in any field; it could also be viewed in terms of how understanding the patriarchal sect is towards the incompetence and insufficiencies that may have been prevailing within the society both within women as well as men or transformation with the fact that we accept the things the way they are, a very traditional way of analyzing that could be biased with some elements of criticism; or analyzing the role of women and their contributions towards societal development; and also a complete revolutionary change in the inherent characteristics of both women and men that may cut across scientific and biological factors that determine the traits of both the gender; and also it is important to dispel the presumption that feminism

*Assistant Professor, LLDIMS,
(Affiliated to Guru Gobind Singh Indraprastha University, Delhi)
** Media Practicener

necessarily brings women together and that only a woman can make efforts towards advancement of the same gender because factors such as envy are in abundance in the softer sex too. How should the contribution of prostitutes and sex-traders be measured in this society? Could there be a scientific justification for that? Should there be a change in the perspectives towards women or men (gigolo) trafficking and how does education help or sometimes corrupts the significance of sexual relationships in the society: how legal or illegal or how ethical or unethical can this be? How does right to speech cuts across the socially constructed feminine norms and manners; are they actually derived from our chromosomes? Does transformation need to be seen through this prism? The role of sex-workers and co-educational backgrounds and working environment have made it necessary to study the discrepancies in laws meant for sexual harassment, discrimination and usual moral policing. It is important to draw a line between sexual exploitation and normal friendly banters and mutual exchanges, pornography and labour laws (as in case of "*Happy Dent advertisement where labour being used as light through their glowing teeth*") and definition of sarcasm and its permissible limit as defined by intellectual property rights in England and other places. How can we distinguish between feminism and feminist or male ego, self-respect, humility and identity generation?

Empowering women and social transformation

Women's empowerment and social transformation has been an old endeavor towards larger and sustainable social development. Transformation may however, have different interpretations. It is important to question what "*power*" and "*transformation*" are and what they ought to be in relation to man-woman-societal dynamics? It can be viewed with a change in the thought processes of men that women are equally competent and not to be mocked at for their output in any field; it could also be viewed in terms of how understanding the patriarchal sect is towards the incompetence and insufficiencies that may have been prevailing within the society both within women as well as men or transformation with the fact that we accept the things the way they are, a very traditional way of analyzing that could be biased with some elements of criticism; or analyzing the role of women and their contributions towards societal development; and also a complete revolutionary change in the inherent characteristics of both women and men that may cut across scientific and biological factors that determine the traits of both the gender; and also it is important to dispel the presumption that feminism necessarily brings women together and that only a woman can make efforts towards advancement of the same gender because factors such as envy are in abundance in the softer sex too. How should the contribution of prostitutes and sex-traders be measured in this society? Could there be a scientific justification for that? Should there be a change in the perspectives towards women or men (gigolo) trafficking and how does education help or sometimes corrupts the significance of sexual relationships in the society: how legal or illegal or how ethical or unethical can this be? How does right to speech cuts across the socially constructed feminine norms and manners; are they actually derived from our chromosomes? Does transformation need to be seen through this prism? The role of sex-workers and co-educational backgrounds and working environment have made it necessary to study the discrepancies in laws meant for sexual harassment, discrimination and usual moral policing. It is important to draw a line between sexual exploitation and normal friendly banters and mutual exchanges, pornography and labour laws (as in case of "*Happy Dent advertisement where labour being used as light through their glowing teeth*") and definition of sarcasm and its permissible limit as defined by intellectual property rights in England and other places. The causes for tagging a girl as a "*Behenji, BTM or L.S.*". How can we distinguish between feminism and feminist or male ego, self-respect, humility and identity generation? Does marriage gives us the license to rape or sexually assault each other-the issue of marital rape? Also an analysis of the evolution and changing role of women along with media. What could be the causes and reasons behind dowry deaths and female foeticide? How do we perceive the right over one's body?

The significance of women in their own as well as societal transformation has been an immensely important issue for understanding socio-political and economic status and dynamics for any state as well as international relations. Feminism is a wing of the Marxist theories as they challenge the prevailing positivist order and do not accept it the way it is. Gender issues highlight the inherent inequalities amongst human beings and their respective perspectives in normal circumstances along with the usual objective differences that are visible to the naked eye. Gender debate may not be always feminism, as described by the "anti-feminists" since both perspectives are equally important to the larger sustainable development and building personalities individually. Male arguments are presumed to be more aggressive and value-free that can be empathized through female arguments and thoughts that are normative and transform the society for the better.

Gender issues with specific reference to educational opportunities, overcoming pressures of sati, widow remarriages and *devdasi (temple dancer or murali)* had been dealt with by pre-colonial thinkers such as Raja Rammohan Roy who played a very significant role through promotion of vernacular languages and freedom of press and right to inheritance of property. Adoption laws in the pre-independence era were found to be gendered as well[1] in the Western part of India. Adoption in this part of our country was considered to be an auspicious rite or ritual in terms of property inheritance that, however, remain confined to boys. Girl child couldn't be adopted and declaired heiress to the property. Only boys were entitled to formal adoption practices in most of the communities save the communities of *"temple-dancer"* and courtesan communities within which the *"prostitutes"* or *"dancing girls"* could follow their mothers profession and inherited her property. During the British rule, *the naikins* formed a community and practiced their own customs of adoption, joint family, inheritance that deviated from the broader Hindu caste community. In 1864s, under the customary laws of *Talabda Kolis* in Gujarat and the Konkan, women were permitted to divorce their husbands and indulge into a contract of a *natra* or secondary marriage despite the former husband being alive and without his or the caste or community's consent. The *Teli (oil-presser)* community of the caste of *Khandesh* awarded a very modern and broad-minded decision of letting the wife Narbada to walk out of her marriage with a man who had acquired leprosy something and to remarry which was in conflict with the normal Hindu marriage laws. Therefore, in some communities women do enjoy better status and rights as compared to the larger Hindu laws. The very sanctity of marriage and sharing of mutual love and problems loses significance in certain situations.

There has to be a distinguishing factor between vernacular languages and customary laws because there have differences within a class, caste and community in their job opportunities particularly during the colonial period. Along with divisions with these structures there have been repeated instances of discriminatory practices against women belonging to different communities. Therefore, it is essential to make a clear demarcation between discrimination and sexual harassment and deliberate over discrepancies in these laws. Discrimination may include several practices such as property laws, inheritance laws, exploitation of the labour or women that may take the form of sexual harassment sometimes but they both can not be fused always. Sexual Harassment can and mostly is viewed along with beauty, appearance and dressing sense of both men and women and may include physical assault such as rape, molestation. Discrimination needs to study the problem of Behenji that may not be always castist and has been discussed in detail within the purview of this paper later. Rape further requires detailed analysis vis-à-vis marriage and rights of husband and wife and the ways in which couples may make love with each other. Oral sex is considered to be unhygienic and may have a very derogatory connotation, interpreted to be animal like and could be a cause for divorce if there is no consent mutually. A certain sect in Christianity may hail oral sex as being sacred[2] Not permitting one's partner to have sexual intercourse could also be a cause for divorce and cause for marital rape as the debate revolves around the fact as to how marriage should be interpreted. There is an age factor or limitation in India after which a woman cannot file a marital rape case against her husband. Marriage is not merely sex and the French version of love is "sharing the same washing machine" but the role of media by means of talk shows and counsellors has been increasing through televisions, radio, newspapers and advertisements and so on. Sexual behaviour as discussed by Michel Foucault, has been stereotyped and also biologically determined and not always determined from feelings or imagination of the people. The problem of marital rape has been dealt with through legal mechanisms in several countries such as France, Spain and around 104 countries. Separation becomes an important clause for filing a case against marital rape but sometimes a woman may be some other kind of pressure not to get separated from her husband or may merely forgive unless things go out of control. The significance of the media and the role of pornographic movies and movies based on extra-marital affairs is an issue of concern whether to promote it or completely discard it. Sexuality and love relationships are also culturally determined that may cut across a woman's freedom of speech and expression[3] as she may be considered to be indecent as there are certain cultural and customary practice of that consider women as an epitome of manners and etiquettes who is expected to blush and depict the softer bit of her to men and society. She cannot confess her love and desires first in practice despite the famous hospitality quote "*ladies first*" along with the elitist definition of feminine etiquettes. In addition to that the Indian constitution through the Articles 15, Article 16 and Article 17 have persistently tried to empower women through economic and social reservations and policies such as economic policies such as single girl child educational policy in India[4] that was meant to provide scholarship opportunities for daughters of parents who just had single girl child as an issue but preferably for professional courses, although it has also been argued that globalisation has promoted "rate of girls" enrolment in secondary schools as well from 36% in 1990 to 61% in 1997 globally. In 2007, the global level of primary school enrolment for girls was 79% which is slowly catching up with that for boys 85%. Educational policies for women may include 5% reservations for women in some colleges under University of Delhi such as Dyaal Singh College and certain minimum marking criteria in some central and state universities in order to push women further. However, according to the World Bank, UNDP, Jubilee Research, 1/6th of the world adults are illiterate and 2/3rd of the world's illiterates are women[5]. Sub-Saharan African women are 100 times likely to die during child-birth as compared to women in high-income OECD countries. Therefore, we do not know how far policies of un-prescribed contraception could be a boon for the continuation of our human race and where and how can we keep a check in order to control the population growth of the world.

J. Ann Tickner[6] argues that feminism as a debate that flourished in 1960s and 1970s that emerged for women to be treated at par with men. The Liberal feminists seek withdrawal of laws and providing larger scope for women in every sphere. The radical feminists or constructivists consider gender as a social construction that promotes male dominance and female subordination; male autonomy and female restrictions; male glorification and female devaluation. Such a gendered arrangement is considered to be a justification for the protection for women that Tickner also discards as a necessity. However, they contradict by arguing that women are exploited by different means of male dominance such as rape both pre as well as post-marital; domestic violence for dowry, money or due to neo-liberal policies that are implemented by the states and international organisations without prioritizing the cause for women. Feminists argue that laws are rigid and maintain status quo and does not adapt to the persistent and periodic changes of the society. It, however, continued to remain unstable in entire South Asia. Job opportunities for women in OECD countries and Western Europe increased to the extent of reduction of job opportunities for men between 1970s-1990s. It was during this phase the prevailing economic crisis was a major cause for concern due to which some of the big companies of the West that had earlier confined the "knowledge intensive" aspect of production process to the West while the "labour intensive" aspect confined to developing countries now sought greater decentralization and managerial flexibility in order to overcome the problems of the Trade Union. The Garment industries along with electronics, toy manufacturing and food processing across Europe and North America who failed to "relocate abroad" opted for the feminization of work force[7]. Gender stratification was observed at the global communication level too as men have been found to be comprising of a large majority of internet users. Late 1990s only *38% of internet users in USA were women; 25% in Brazil; 16% in Russia; and 4% in Arab countries*[8]. New media technologies have made women more vulnerable to cyber crimes and other types of crimes such as web-based pornography, entrapment via e-mail, and offensive text messaging. Pornography has several cultural connotations as sarcasm has different laws for adjudication in England and in India too. Pornography women and art has been the hallmark of Indian culture in the form of architectural designs Ajanta Ellora and paintings. However, nude paintings of Goddess Saraswati made by M.F. Hussain were criticized in the name of religion. Advertisements play a very significant role in picturising the image of women in promoting products such as condoms and sanitary napkins has both positive and negative connotations. Some people within a friend circle love sharing pornographic popularly known as "*non-veg jokes*" that could be abusing and should be stopped mutually and not blown out proportion amongst friend circle. One can argue that one has right over one's own body and therefore may be comfortable in featuring in the advertisements. The definition of beauty has been changing for women also through the media where beauty paegents are given so much hype and become a cause fro depression amongst teenagers who get obsessed about their bodies. The classical concept of beauty prefers curves and not an extensively measured figure of any woman as DaVinci puts a fit and healthy man into a fixed measured box to identify it with a proper human body. Sexist languages have been found to be very common within mass media. Women are widely seen to be working even in the global information and communication sector as news readers along with engineers, global retailing and global finance. Increase in trade has helped in reduction of wage inequalities between women and men in Bangladesh but has led to widened gap in Zambia. High salaried jobs are still occupied by men. Kiran Bedi was not selected for the post of Police Commissioner of Delhi and a man was selected instead despite all her efforts to reform the judicial custody standards and promoting education and harnessing different skills for prisoners. Every individual may have some limitations or capacities within them because no one is self-sufficient and it is an interdependent society and therefore one has to be patient and have to be understanding.

Due to rising economic crisis between 1980s-1990s many people opted out of the "formal sector" and preferred working in the "informal sector" that include "sex workers, trans-world markets, mail-order brides"[9]. Ann Tickner further discusses the causes of sex-workers and how they are being used and exploited by the state to control the army. The United Nations bans human trafficking however, the role of sex workers in a normal life could be interesting if there is consent from the sex-worker herself. The UN had put forth a Convention for the Suppression of Traffic in Persons and the Exploitation of the Prostitution of Others which was approved by the General Assembly in 1949 but has so far been ratified by only 70 states.

Biologically, a man may face difficulty in controlling his sexual desires as the blood flow and adrenaline and other hormones may push a man towards premature or not rationally judged sexual relationship that may not always be love and a woman may due to various reasons not be in a situation to indulge in such an intercourse all the time. This kind of a debate may lead to cases of marital rapes. However, biological problems can not permit harassments and abuses to continue. Therefore, women trafficking and role of sex-workers may prove to be significant if they do not lead to an imbalance in the proper family life in the form of adultery and bigamy. Proper documentation prior to women trafficking could be proposed by countries that promote state-driven sex trading. Women have the right over their body and may declare their consent to such relationships without later indulging in blackmailing and other criminal activities. Rape therefore requires deeper analysis of the rapist if he has been denied such feelings or intercourse at home. and their utility in promoting international terrorism and wars. Society in Bosnia permits rape of any Muslim woman as a purification practice[10]. This creates a conflict between state and inter and intra customary laws and ethics. State can not practice sexual atrocities on the masses. It is not clear how one may perceive the concept of secularism[11] and sexual harassment in such places. Police and violence inflicted by army has been heinous in the north-eastern regions of India and Kashmir under the garb of maintaining security for the masses. The justification given is the long time spent by army-men at the battlefield or the border without sufficient breaks, remuneration and contact with their families. The plight of their legitimate families has never been explored by the media. Media does not exercise the rationality to make their observations more acceptable to the people that would prevent mass violence against mis-interpretations and also cause embarrassment for a rape victim. It is the "new social movements" that have contributed to the cause of women's empowerment but the media, as Harvey may define it to have contributed to the "time-space compression" in terms of spreading of information about such movements and developments. The "*Immoral Traffic (Prevention) Act, 1956*" that was amended in 1986, has been having negative impact on prostitutes as any woman walking on the streets at night may be arrested by the police[12]. In order to overcome the problems of unfair arrests of women at night our government formed a law commission that proposed a bill that prohibited policemen from touching any woman and her statements should be recorded with her relatives, friend or any representative of any women's organisations. Any police officer who refuses to abide by his duties of filing case when any woman is raped then he is liable to be punished provided the policeman's offence should be reported by the victim or the people. However, in case of doubt it is unfair to stop a lady policeman to catch a possible prostitute on the street during late night hours. In a decision taken by the Supreme Court presiding over Mathura Case[13], the powers of the media was curtailed by forcing the press not to publish anything related to a rape trial which is non-bailable. Media plays a very significant role in generating mass awareness about people. Any woman's background is extremely important to adjudicate on cases of rape and sexual harassment. This law seems to be presuming that men cannot, rather would not indulge in prostitution either in the form of gigolos themselves or pimps who act as the third party in promoting sex-trade and callgirl activities. Some well established women either in the field of academics or a socialite with lot of financial might or position in the society may force any man or seduce any man to indulge in sexual relationship with her without the man's consent. It is misuse of any kind of power and needs to be explored further.

Just before Christmas, the Taranaki District Health Board in New Zealand announced its plans to make the emergency contraceptive pill freely available through pharmacies for youth age 12 to 24. The pill was already available through agencies like Family Planning NZ, but the cost without a prescription is non-negligible at about USD$40. The announcement produced rather predictable and boring reactions from both supporters and critics. Given the recent debates in the U.S., it might be a good time (a) to provide policymakers a framework within which to ponder the question; and (b) to cite some evidence on the most pertinent questions that come up while pondering[14]. This policy seems to help states to promote sex-workers and prostitutes and adolescent teenagers to indulge in pre-marital sexual relationships because men may find it biologically necessary to have one although they may not be serious about a long-term commitment leading to even long term psychological trauma for which neither the man nor a woman or a young teenager maybe prepared. There could be increase in gender related violence and HIV/AIDS because of this policy. Moreover, biologically it could prove to be fatal for a woman's health too. We cannot presume that such policies are meant for family planning practices since they are open to young teenagers. The World Bank one of the pillars of neo-liberal economic policies have been contributing more than $1 billion on women's education and training since 1995, an amount that has increased manifold since 1980s. Birth control pills prescribed by doctors is a very polished way of promoting sex and sex-trading amongst people as they say they are not mentally prepared to plan out a family yet. It is just sex and no love-making in such a transactions turning doctors into mere pimps.

Feminists have challenged that there is no proper Jurisprudence and have criticized the notion that women's rights are unfair, individualistic and driven by self-interests. Law is expected to define the culture, values, attitudes, expectations and presumptions of the dominant culture that is projected as universally applicable. Feminists like post-modernists argue context is very important for legislation so that cultural diversities and customary laws. Scholars have distinguished between two types of human conduct and behaviour: rational that is necessarily presumed to be a male trait and women considered to be unreasonable. The phase of neo-liberalism and dominance of utilitarian economics has affected womens' lives a lot. Women play a major biological role in conceiving an infant that in the long-run adds to the larger work force of any country and nation since it has been argued by Kautilya, Plato and other economists that population helps deriving recognition to any state or society. Women traditionally have been playing a dual role in the larger societal and family development by carrying out responsibilities of the household thereby reducing the burden and responsibilities of men who have to act as the bread-earner for the family. They maintain the division of labour and work within the family that gets overlooked by the economic calculations of the international and state organisations. This prevents the women from getting any kind of remuneration for their dual contribution if they are working outside. In certain employment areas women have been treated unfairly in terms of wages and employment since the notion of "*equal pay for equal work*" being a directive principle is non-justiciable in India and at the global sphere women were being paid less for a long time in the world of sports such as Tennis, Cricket and athletics and also other entertainment industry (in modeling however men may get paid lesser than women because beauty is gendered and revolves around women in general) because sports are necessarily considered to be meant for men and that sports becomes a completely discreationary choice that may not have a contribution or relevance for the economic growth of any country and society. Nevertheless, scientifically sports may help in building healthy population and work force that supports Darwinian thought that a fit society is a necessity. The problem of wages and employment are calculated through the "Labour force Participation Ratio (LFPR)" for both men and women[15]. LFPR is the ratio of actual labour cost to the working population. Earlier contribution of women labour was not clearly visible through this ratio particularly in the rural areas, however, schemes such as the National Rural Employment Act (NREGA) has been playing a very crucial role in states such as Rajasthan for the upliftment of both rural unemployed men and women. However, domestic helps and maids who have been working in private homes for washing clothes, utensils, mopping and cooking work in Suri, Birbhum district of West Bengal are not permitted to avail the government allowance they get under the NREGA. The working maids in this district complain that the amount they get under NREGA is insufficient for the family. Feminists criticize the Rational Choice Theory of state that presumes that state policies are already rational and cover the entire population and their needs. In addition to the problems of employment and wages women have been facing atrocities due to their respective class, caste and religious backgrounds. However, women's employment have been on the rise since 1980s and 1990s, in the era of globalisation: 14% in North America; 76% in East and Central Europe. In 1970s Microchip Production gained immense importance with respect to recruitment of women workers at cheap wages. Unmarried and young women were hired at very low wages and complaining women were dismissed from the jobs[16]. It has not been discussed in the literature whether these hired women were engineers who had just completed their engineering degrees that is why they were young and unmarried and also the issues they complained about. Transport is one of most important issues women complain about along with security. Along with highly skilled and educated jobs that require professionals and technicians have come up which require high levels of skills, confidence and ability; labour intensive sectors, low skilled jobs and part-time jobs have also come up as an outcome of globalisation. Nursing, data processing, personal services, call centres, home helping and so on are a few examples of such new types of job opportunities. Jobs have been increased in the state health-sector and education sector or social services have also been created as they have been sub-contracted private agencies. Most part-time jobs taken up by women labour market offers very little to them. 45% of part time jobs in Germany, United Kingdom and Japan have been occupied by women along with larger proportion of professional and managerial posts. Women are also provided with maternity leaves and men are entitled for paternity leaves a way of expressing a mutual and shared responsibility as a family towards reproduction, child rearing and upbringing. Women are free to be more flexible in terms of careers if they get proper support from their families her own parents and husband and in-laws both in case of success as well as failures and crisis. She can expect support from her family and in-laws to pursue what she aspires and accept each other the way they are overcoming problems of ego, both male and female, and think constructively in terms of family and someone of one's own. That can symbolize a perfect man and a woman. Feminism can not be misused by being haughty and excessively egoistic either. Societal transformation has to be analysed with different viewpoints: transformation could be carried out through several means, by increasing participation for women in political bodies; Transformation may however, have different interpretations. It is important to question what "power" and "transformation" are and what they ought to be in relation to man-woman-societal dynamics? Transformation should be focused on how to balance male and female ego which is completely psychological and may not always be negatively interpreted to be in relation to career and superiority complex but understanding and respecting each other's feelings and sentiments to the fullest. Concept of surrogacy and *In vitro Fertilised* (IVF) pregnancies should be promoted for those who have some physical and biological problems. In case selective breeding or eugenics is preferred as suggested by Plato then it could be psychologically fatal for the partner who may feel demeaned and belittled.

It can be viewed with a change in the thought processes of men that women are equally competent and not to be mocked at for their output in any field; it could also be viewed in terms of how understanding the patriarchal sect is towards the incompetence and insufficiencies that may have been prevailing within the society both within women as well as men or transformation with the fact that we accept the things the way they are, a very traditional way of analyzing that could be biased with some elements of criticism; or analyzing the role of women and their contributions towards societal development; and also a complete revolutionary change in the inherent characteristics of both women and men that may cut across scientific and biological factors that determine the traits of both the gender; and also it is important to dispel the presumption that feminism necessarily brings women together. It has been observed on several occasions that a woman herself may be vengeful and driven by envy. The significance of women in "social transformation" is an immensely important issue for understanding socio-political and economic status and dynamics for any country. Feminism is a wing of Marxist theories. They challenge the prevailing positivist approach to the study of society, the world and international system and society. The problem of low members of women in public office, currently at a global average of just 16.7% in national assemblies, to enable public decision-making under the United Nations Fund for Women (UNIFEM) supports efforts to increase share of women that are elected into office. In 2007, UNIFEM had supported organisations in Sierra Leone to ensure that the media code of the conduct for the election incorporated strong anti-discrimination elements to ensure that woman candidates received the same amount of quality of coverage men. UNIFEM worked extensively on upcoming or recent elections in Burundi, Cambodia, Kenya, Nigeria and Sierra Leone. It works with political parties encouraging nomination of women leaders as candidates for office. It also supports to enable political parties to incorporate national priorities on gender equality in their campaign platforms and legislative agendas, to nominate gender equality in their campaign platforms and legislative agendas, and to nominate gender equality advocates as candidates for office. After elections, UNIFEM seek to build capacity of voters to demand gender equality policies of selected officials, an approach currently being piloted in Nepal and Kenya, with 'Women's Election Watch' groups tracking and assessing the legislative performance of politicians. However, it is not clear by what means does this body carry out this performance of assessing the performance of the politicians. UNIFEM has worked alongside ministries of woman's affairs in Afghanistan, Algeria, Argentina, Columbia, Democratic Republic of the Congo, Ecuador, Jamaica, Montenegro, Morocco, Paraguay, Serbia, South Africa, Uruguay, Venezuela and Zimbabwe, and the occupied Palestinian territory, to help resolve issues such as ambiguities about the role of these ministries, and inadequate positioning, staffing and resources.

In Argentina, UNIFEM is partnering with the *Fundacion Mujeres en Igualda* (an UNIFEM guantee) on a project that seeks to organize and mobilize women to promote transparency and promote citizens' rights of access to information. UNIFEM is partnering with *United Nations Development Program (UNDP) and the Non-governmental Organisations (NGO), Gender At Work,* to develop 5 year global initiative aimed at improving the quality of governance from the perspective of women's capacity to access public services, and to demand accountability for poor quality services and failures to deliver. The programme had to be implemented in 6 to 10 countries. In 2006 UNIFEM supported inclusion of gender equality provisions in the development of new constitutions in Bolivia, Iraq, Montenegro, and Thailand and the interim constitutions of Nepal and Sudan. It further supported the removal of discriminatory provisions from legislation and policies in Burundi, Ecuador, Liberia and Nepal and provided technology and financial support to strengthen woman's rights and gender equality laws and elsewhere and fighting against all forms of sexual harassment. It also played a very important role in establishing daughters' rights to inherit family land in Nepal and removal of discriminatory provisions in HIV/AIDS laws in Ecuador. It promotes greater women participation in peace negotiations and peace-building processes. Burundi UNIFEM not only arranged for women to participate as observers in the Arusha talks but subsequently supported women to ensure a constitutional quota for women's political participation. Sudan UNIFEM supported women's access to the first and third consortiums to ensure that women's views were heard on the implementation of the comprehensive peace agreement. In Liberia, UNIFEM encouraged voter registration for women supporting organisations that provided physical transportation for those who lived far from polling stations or who could not, for other reasons, register to vote. This body further assesses the judicial review proceedings of different countries. However, UNIFEM still has a modest annual budget of only $35 million. The Nordic countries have the highest rates of female membership of parliaments in the world and have almost the highest levels of female employment. In Arab Countries, women comprise merely 3.8% of parliamentarians and thus women's employment as a percentage of men's is 38.6% which is the lowest for any region of the world. Judicial bodies and proceedings have also played a very significant role in overcoming problems of sexual harassment at workplace through an internationally signed Convention supported by the United Nations General Assembly in 1979. India became signatory to this *Convention on the Elimination of All Forms of Discrimination against Women (CEDAW)*[17].

The United Nations has created an indicator called the Gender Development Index (GDI) in order to measure state development along with the Human Development Index (HDI). However, the GDI too, overlooks the domestic contributions of women and restricts its focus on literacy, life expectancy, school enrolment, and income disaggregated by gender. There could be a valid justification behind the domestic contribution being excluded from the parameters within the GDI and HDI, women may hire domestic help for regular domestic practices and crèches where they may leave their children during their office hours where they are taken care of by someone else for food and playing time with other children. Sweden and now many countries have been providing the facilities of crèches for women within their workplace premises. However, on several occasions maids and crèches have been proved to be fatal for the upbringing of children in various forms. Nevertheless, domestic factors ought to be included as a parameter because they sometimes lead to problems of domestic violence and not all families may be able to afford such kind of help all the time or during any family crisis a family may have to cut down on expenses that may include cutting down on expenses on domestic maid and crèches. Home-based works and the rights of such workers and their contribution to economic earning have been recognized by the *International Labour Organisation ILO's Homework Convention in 1996*[18]. International Organisations particularly the economic organisations have been criticized in terms of policies they put forth such as the public utility zones and are called the Special Economic Zones (SEZs) that are exempted from taxes for being inefficient in providing security and sufficient remuneration to laborers particularly women.

Excess of sports and household work may be hazardous for women for their biological reproductive role and anatomical differences from men due to which labour oriented work may be fatal in the long run. However, it has been observed that men have respected their countries with feminist connotations "Her" and therefore, requires protection but the atrocities on women in general have been criticized for being contradictory to patriotism and nationalistic sentiments. Women are either derogated for being incompetent for a certain kind of job but sometimes it may be interpreted with elitist interpretation. Eliticism is interpreted in terms of class distinctions such as aristocracy or nobility or royalty or chivalry whereby, women are meant to be served that are being overlooked by some feminist and linguistic scholars with reference to hospitality etiquettes such as *"ladies first"* or *"behind every successful man there is a woman"* and in restaurants where waiters may pull-up a chair for the lady who visits for an outing and they or other men in any gathering may bow to greet you. Women, too have become habitual with such behavioral etiquettes that they expect the same in every situation[19] due to which women in India find it uncomfortable and deplorable the behaviour they get from the policemen and army either on the streets or when they independently approach the police for any kind of help. Transformation in some instances seems peculiar as in some parts of our cities in India some girls or a certain section of the crowd has to face a kind of name calling such as Behenji or *Behenji Turned Modern (BTM)* or *Dehati or L.S.*. This section of the crowd is not lagging behind from the objectively elitist sections of our society neither are they all the time caste driven. They have a fine living standard with all the modern appliances such as air conditioners, microwave ovens and outings at the most popular and pompous shopping malls or McDonalds or Ansal Plaza for a Valentine Day date with their partners in Delhi. They celebrate birthday parties, use cellphones, can read English and pursuing English medium education, use online shopping facilities and wear western formals too[20]. Quoting some of our true observations and incidents as a student of Deshbandhu College, University of Delhi Kalkaji, New Delhi, this unusual kind of discrimination is difficult to interpret and to convert it into a compulsion to remove the same. A college *freshers' party organized by a group of students with Sharma (a north indian Brahmin boy from Uttar Pradesh and a very good student brought up in Najafgarh region of Delhi), Mittal (a non-Brahmin north Indian and a decent student brought up in Delhi), a Nair (a Malyali girl, brought up in Delhi and a good student but suffered a slump in some papers and fluent in English too), Das (bengali non-brahmin category who is herself dark complexioned but had no hesitation in mocking at a dark complexioned boy) and us*[21] for the juniors with a similar diverse crowd was not attended (out of embarrassment because of pre-conceived ideas and Behenji tag about Deshbandhu College and its crowd) by a *Pandey girl (a Brahmin from Uttar Pradesh, North India, brought up in Delhi) and a Chauhan (a Rajput, brought up in Delhi).* Smoking of *cigarettes* by upper class academicians and socialites and *bidi*[22] amongst the roadside sweepers and domestic helps and domestic helps both male and females creates an elitist divide in the society that may be casteist but sometimes not and sometimes completely out of differences in their purchasing capacities. There was unity in diversity observed in both the above mentioned groups: Sharma et al who invited Pandey et al for the party despite caste and region distinctions in both along with an intra-caste and region ignorance since Sharma and Pandey were both North Indian Brahmin from Uttar Pradesh. In another incident, a Brahmin girl pursuing masters in Political Science (2006-2008) Hindi Medium, from *Gargi College (for girls), University of Delhi,* was a decently dressed nice looking (no coloured complexion problem with her) brilliant student and extremely efficient in translating on the spot the English lectures delivered in the classroom into Hindi. She had no trouble understanding English lectures for papers such as International Relations for which they seldom got translated material to read. However, there were some Yadav despite being Delhiites were Hindi medium students too were the same as the Brahmin girl. However, the topper in this batch was an Aggarwal girl from Bhopal who only pursued her graduation, masters and M.Phil/Phd in Political Science (English medium) from Lady Sriram College, University of Delhi, can not in anyway called a Behenji. She never looked like or behaved like one. However, it is very difficult to define the Behenji behaviour save certain distinctions such as the colours they may choose or the designs on their clothings may be too flashy and not confined to bright but too much filling for some as compared the simple, sobre and subtle colours; or something that they may wear or use that they can not carry themselves confidently like others but still they do make pizzas. A housewife of a Chaurasia family in Delhi has been grooming a three year old son and simultaneously pursuing her graduation in English Medium from the countryside. This section of the society wear the latest trends in clothings too such as pyjamas, parallels, night gown and night suits and listen to western music at home and an unmarried girl also pursuing a separate course in multimedia along with her graduation through correspondence.

Transformation further requires detailed study since there is an inherent jealousy within the feminine sect globally vis-à-vis beauty, social status, performance, male friends and boyfriends. A girl may several times refuse to take help in the form of books or social and family interactions even if she is invited from some other girl but may have no problem if the same help is offered to her from any male counterpart or competitor. It could be healthy in a way since she and her mind may want a male partner in life or have some family problems that may be terribly disturbing or some negative experiences with some other female friend who was not worth being a friend and was jealous herself and may be envious or demeaning only towards her female counterparts who may or not be a lesbian and could be a good friend. In such a complex relationship women may be vengeful towards the other women and particularly the one who is close to her as a friend or some other relationship but the closeness is still driven by envy, and therefore, inflict the pain that she may have suffered earlier not always with the intention of making the other woman stronger or make her realize the challenges of life that the latter may not have faced and has had a better life style as compared to the former (atleast how the former perceives it to be) but simply out of envy.

However, feminists challenge such polished behavioral implications as women are prevented from decision-making procedures even in a normal family or household work. Despite that the monarchical governance through female monarch support the elitist definition of women. Woman is considered to be a guardian of purity[23]. In the concept of marriage there is a practiced hierarchy where the bride-taker is superior to the bride-giver. And it is further argued that the *concepts* of *anuloma* and pratiloma marriages reduce the status of women in a particular *castist* order: *anuloma* is the marriage between an upper caste boy and a lower caste girl; and pratiloma is the marriage between woman of ritually pure groups with men of lower ritual status. Stringent punishments have been awarded to those who have violated these norms. Scientifically it has been proved that it is the father of the child who is responsible for the sex of the child and not the mother despite that there has been less awareness amongst people and there have been cases of immense torture against women for having given birth to a girl child and anxieties over the streedhan and dowry that has to be piled up during the course of the upbringing of the girl child. A woman is entitled to gifts and presents and propertied gifts both during and before marriage from her parents. Traditionally and historically our Vedas have been biased against women. The legal codes provided by Manu provided a legal and ideological principles that consider women as demeaning as the lower and the lowest castes in the Indian society that is yet to change completely in our routined lifestyle.

Footnote

1. Sturman, Rachel.2012. "Ch.3 Hindu Law as a Regime of Rights".in.The Government of Social Life in Colonial India:Liberalism, Religious Law and Women's Rights.CUP.p.p.143
2. Hegel
3. Article 19 Right to Freedom of Speech and Expression
4. This policy was stalled by the Supreme Court after a PIL filed by people calling this policy to be unfair.
5. Hobden, Stephen and Richard Wyn Jones.2008. "Ch. 8 Marxist Theories of International Relations".in.The Globalisation of

World Politics: An Introduction to International Relations 4e.John Baylis, Steve Smith and Patricia Owens.OUP.p.p.146

6. Tickner, J.Ann.2008. "Ch. 15 Gender in world politics".in.The Globalisation of World Politics: An Introduction to International Relations 4e.John Baylis, Steve Smith and Patricia Owens.OUP.p.p.264-277
7. Steans, Jill.2000. "Ch. 35 The Gender Dimension".in.The Global Transformations Reader: An Introduction to the Globalisation Debate.ed.Anthony McGrew and David Held.Polity Press Blackwell Publishing Ltd.,p.p.336-373
8. Ibid..6
9. Ibid..6
10. Ibid..4
11. Ashish Nandy ....Secularism
12. Agnes, Flavia.. "Ch. 15 Protecting Women against Violence?: Review of a decade of legislation, 1980-1989".in.State and Politics in India.p.p.521-525
13. Ibid..7
14. Should Your Government Provide Free Emergency Contraception to Girls? (Development Impact blog, World Bank, Jan.28)
15. Sen, Sunanda.Ethical basis of Feminist Economics: A challenge to the neo-liberal agenda, a case study on Bangladesh
16. Mehta, Jaya.Women and Globalisation.http://www.revolutionarydemoc.org/rdv5n2/womglob.htm
17. Ibid..4 and The Vishakha Judgment
18. Ibid..4,10
19. A group of M.Phil scholars (batch 2008-2011)from The Centre for the study of Law and Governance, Jawaharlal Nehru University, New Delhi, carried out a course survey on

discrimination and harassment of women and collected data from University of Delhi and JNU.

20. Ibid.,19

21. Chaturvedi, Shweta (a Brahmin girl from Uttar Pradesh) and Shreya Chakrabarty (Brahmin girl from Bengal) but both brought up in Delhi

22. Cigarette bidi smoking observation was further confirmed by our College faculty Dr. Joyeeta Dutta

23. Desai, Neera and Maithreyi Krishnaraj. "Ch.12 An Overview of the Status of Women in India".in.Status of Women.p.p.296-319

Bibliography:

Agnes, Flavia.. "Ch. 15 Protecting Women against Violence?: Review of a decade of legislation, 1980-1989".in.State and Politics in India.p.p.521-525

Desai, Neera and Maithreyi Krishnaraj. "Ch.12 An Overview of the Status of Women in India".in.Status of Women.p.p.296-319

Hobden, Stephen and Richard Wyn Jones.2008. "Ch. 8 Marxist Theories of International Relations".in.The Globalisation of World Politics: An Introduction to International Relations 4e.John Baylis, Steve Smith and Patricia Owens.OUP.p.p.146

Mehta, Jaya.Women and Globalisation.
http://www.revolutionarydemoc.org/rdv5n2/womglob.htm

Sen, Sunanda.Ethical basis of Feminist Economics: A challenge to the neo-liberal agenda, a case study on Bangladesh

Steans, Jill.2000. "Ch. 35 The Gender Dimension".in.The Global Transformations Reader: An Introduction to the Globalisation Debate.ed.Anthony McGrew and David Held.Polity Press Blackwell Publishing Ltd.,p.p.336-373

Sturman, Rachel.2012. "Ch.3 Hindu Law as a Regime of Rights".in.The Government of Social Life in Colonial

India:Liberalism, Religious Law and Women's Rights.CUP.p.p.143

Tickner, J.Ann.2008. "Ch. 15 Gender in world politics".in.The Globalisation of World Politics: An Introduction to International Relations 4e.John Baylis, Steve Smith and Patricia Owens.OUP.p.p.264-277

Convergent Journalism: A Step Towards Future Multimedia Integration

Dr. Suresh Chandra Nayak*

More is being asked of prospective broadcast journalists today than ever before. Increasingly, successful job seekers will need to be backpack journalists - not just writing and voicing stories, but shooting and editing them as well. While predecessors wrote for television and radio,but now ones broadcast position will likely also involve blogging or interacting on several media.The responsibility grows day by day on the shoulders of the upcoming Journalists. The dictionary meaning of convergence is the combination of two or more things for creativeness. Each every sector uses the latest technologies to keep in tune with the latest trends so as to survive in this competitive world. The meaning of convergence evolved during the 1960s and 1970s when the U.S Department of Defense (DOD) began work with researchers and universities to develop the networked system now known as Internet. The storage of data digitally increased the possibilities of integrating information. When co-operation occurs between print and broadcast for the delivery of multimedia content through the use of computers and the internet is known as convergence.

Asst. Professor, *FMeS, MRIU*

In today's world, each and every thing is changing very fast. We have to keep pace with the changing situations to face the future. Here we can discuss some forms of convergence identified by Prof.Rich Gordon of North Western University. Ownership convergence relates to arrangements within one large media company that encourage cross-promotion and content sharing among print, online, and TV platforms owned by the same company. Tactical convergence describes the content-sharing arrangements and partnerships that have arisen among media companies with separate ownership. Structural convergence associated with changes in news gathering and distribution. A decision to employ a team of multimedia producers and editors to package print material for TV can be the best example of structural convergence. Information- gathering convergence focuses on multiple skills of a reporter.

Mass media plays a predominant role in shaping the future of a nation. We are staying in a tech-savvy world where technology dominates each and every sphere of life. Indian newspapers are becoming 24-news providers just as like broadcast organizations were becoming "24 - hour information engines". Media diversification is the past, digital convergence is the present and multimedia integration is the future. Almost all major newspapers of the world have started accepting multimedia as the brand oriented super power for the newspapers. Both the national and regional dailies of India have started e-publication of their respective newspapers. In this context it's apt to discuss the advantages of each medium of communication. Print media is a portable and a permanent medium of communication. One can carry or keep it wherever he/she moves. TV and Radio is an immediate and emotional medium of communication because of its immediacy in news dissemination. The listeners and viewers feel it as their own because they directly watch the incidents on the screen so, there is a great saying 'a picture is worth than one thousand words'. Online Journalism is regarded as the better of the two worlds because it offers the immediacy of TV and Radio. It's easy to use and interactive.

Each and every medium has its own unique features and drawbacks but each of them try to get hold the attention of the audience. It's the future which can determine the competency of these medium. In a nutshell we can say that convergence is the need of the hour. In the Contemporary Media scenario, the role of Media is paramount. Being a journalist, one has to learn and inculcate the latest new media technologies. Today's Mass Media integrate and imbibe the latest technologies in their organizations so as to keep pace with the changing world scenario. The era of 'Glocalisation' has begun and communication is much easier than ever before. Mc Luhan pertinently coined the word "Global village".

In general, convergence is a coming together of two or more distinct entities or phenomena. Convergence is increasingly prevalent in the IT world; in this context the term refers to the combination of two or more different technologies in a single device. Taking pictures with a cell phone and surfing the Web on a television are two of the most common examples of this trend.

Convergence may influence consumers to accept new technologies. According to some studies, people who aren't computer literate are more likely to embrace the Internet, video-on-demand, and so on. In general, TV is a familiar and non-threatening medium of communication. Displays are large and TVs are easy to operate, requiring almost no training. Personal computers, in spite of their graphical user interfaces tend to be more text-oriented, highly interactive. Computers can be very challenging to use and usually require formal education or a certain personal learning curve. Computer and TV convergence is already underway with Web TV, which pipes the World Wide Web to a slightly-modified TV set with a set-top box from an ordinary phone line and provides a degree of interactivity. A number of interactive games designed for the TV environment can also be played over the Internet. Broadcasting companies such as NBC have partnered with computer companies such as Microsoft for TV program content.

A major barrier to more rapid convergence is the large investment required to bring cable TV to households, both by cable access providers and individual households. Satellite wireless service is another approach that is only beginning to bring its subscriber's access to the Internet. Digital Subscriber Line (DSL) technologies offer the possibility of sufficient bandwidth connections over ordinary phone wires for streaming video to TV sets.

A consortium of leading computer and telecommunication companies including Compaq, IBM, and Microsoft are working towards common standards that will help speed up convergence and hope to sponsor a standard for a relatively low-cost digital TV. They have endorsed a subset of the recommendations of the Advanced Television System Committee (ATSC) that would speed up a transition to digital TV and so that personal computers could have the ability to receive digital video and data.

Our Technological convergence is the trend of technologies to merge into new technologies that bring together a myriad of media. While historically, technology handled one medium or accomplished one or two tasks, through technological convergence, devices are now able to present and interact with a wide array of media.

In the past, for example, each entertainment medium had to be played on a specific device. Video was played on a television by using a video player of some sort, music was played on a tape deck or compact disc player, radio was played on an AM/FM tuner, and video games were played through a console of some sort. Similarly, different communication media used their own technologies. Voice conversation was carried on using a telephone, video communication briefly used high-end video phones, facsimile copies used fax machines, and e-mail used a computer.

Technological convergence in the last few years has resulted in devices that not only interact with the media they are primarily designed to handle, but also with a number of other formats. For example, the Xbox video game console has as its primary purpose the playing of console games, but it is also able to play back video and music and to connect to the Internet. Similarly, most modern DVD players are capable not only of playing DVDs, but also of playing music CDs, displaying photos from photo CDs, playing encoded video in formats such as DIVX or VCD, and playing DVD music.

Technological convergence also leads to devices that are designed specifically to replace a number of different devices. The Apple iPod, for example, while originally conceived of as a portable music player, is now touted equally as a portable video player, photo album, and radio tuner. Cell phones, as well, have moved far beyond their beginnings as simple voice communication devices and now offer the functionality of personal music players, digital cameras, and text messenger systems as well.

The Internet is perhaps the most widespread example of technological convergence. Virtually all entertainment technologies - from radio to television to video to books to games can be viewed and played online. Communications technologies can be used, with the Internet replacing fax machines, telephones, video phones, and the postal service. While technological convergence gives consumers the convenience of having many devices all in one, saving on both size and cost, there is an initial trade off in quality. When technological convergence first gives birth to a new multi-technology, the various technologies it is comprised of are usually at a slightly lower standard than independent devices. Usually within a year or two, however, this disparate quality is reduced to a virtually unnoticeable level.

Convergence can be viewed as the window of opportunity for traditional media to align itself with technologies of the 21st century. The digitization of media and information technology is the major impetus behind convergence (Gershon, 2000).Convergence is the need of the hour. Traditional Folk forms should be disseminated through various mass media agencies than only the message can be disseminated perfectly to the target audience. The future of Journalism is technically more multimedia oriented.

References

Rich Gordon, "Convergence Defined," in Digital Journalism: Emerging Media and the changing Horizons of Journalism, ed.Kevin Kawamoto, 2003.

Quinn, S. (2005a) Convergent Journalism: The Fundamentals of Multimedia Reporting. New York: Peter Lang.

Singer, J.B. (2004), Strange Bedfellows? The diffusion of convergence in four news organizations. Journalism Studies, 5(1), 3-18.

Killebrew, K.C. (2005) Managing Media Convergence: Pathways to Journalistic Cooperation. Ames, Ia.: Blackwell.

Klinenberg, E. (2005) Convergence: News production in a digital age. Annals of the American Academy of Political and Social Science, 597(1), 48-64.

Dailey, L.; Demo, L.; Spillman, M. (2005) The Convergence Continuum: A Model for Studying

Collaboration Between Media Newsrooms. Atlantic Journal of Communication, 13(3), 150-168.

www.wiseGeek.com

Email.id: Suresh.fmes@mriu.edu.in, or

sureshchandranayak1@gmail.com

Cell.no-8010235517, 9555691393

Comment by Sarvesh Dutt Tripathi

Even a child of modern age knows well about the convergence that has been discussed by Dr. Nayak. Dr Dharmendra, it is your discretion whether include it or not or decide what is scholastic in it.

Indian Democracy and New Media

Surya Prakash*

Introuduction

We in India often look upon media as some kind of a valiant mission as an instrument of change, rather than a profession, a value neutral mechanism .Moment changes have griped the world in the past 2 to 3 decade in the entire field, leading to fresh the debates on the nature of democracy, socialism, market technology, environment and other questions.

The most important event has been the so called new industries (a misnomer) or the scientific and technological revolution (STR) and the ICR or the information and communication revolution... they have begun a new era in world history and impact every world of society. Collapse of socialist regimes in the UUSR(??) and Eastern Europe in early 1990s raised several new issues and reopened many others. They put question marks on several concepts thought to have been settled by history.

Nature of socialism, of how to build a new society and how not to, the state, bureaucracy and party, role of parties and classes, of democracy and dissent, freedom of mass media, freedom

Asstt. Professor
Makhanlal Chaturvedi National University of Journalism and Communication,(Noida campus) C-56.A/5 sector 62 Noida

expression, right of the masses and many other questions posed themselves afresh in the socialism.

Questions related with the ownership means of production and communication and of new productive forces have to be posed afresh and solved in different environment. It is clear that era of old types of revolution have passed and new features have emerged. Concept of socialism its self needs networking

A new working class is coming into being and the old concepts about it have to be given up. The nature of imperialism and old concepts about to it has to be given up. The nature of imperialism has to be thought.STR and ICR need thorough study.

The world in fact is passing through giant structural and consciousness related changes, churning the whole world and Indian society. Nothing existing remains intact and the new is being created every moment. We are truly fortunate to be living through and be witness to such extra ordinary transformations.

Social and level of means of production

In India we have a powerful and deep rooted democratic system and institutions of course with all its drawbacks and deficiencies. But it is precisely because of that we fight for improvement of parliamentary mass democratic institutions and not for dismantling. In this sense we go far beyond the traditional interpretation on Marxism of destruction or smashing of state machinery. We certainly create a new state by improving the existing one by and through continuous and general shifts in balance of forces within existing rate. This is the crux of democratic revolution of India in present day world and Indian scenario.

Struggle for democracy has been part and parcel of India's freedom struggle and post independence India. Struggle for democratic rights is an alienable part of prolonged process of democratic revolution in India.

Indian Situation

India today has a strong parliamentary system, open press and media, widespread democratic rights, legal system of parties and organizations and struggles, and a systematic structure of democratic polity going down to village panchayat levels.

In other words, we have all the tools and institutions of democratic and socialist revolution. India is the only country in the world to have given the rights of universal franchise to all the adults on the stroke of pen in 26 January 1950, irrespective of class, caste, gender, educational, economic and other considerations.

This is unprecedented in the world history and it is playing a crucial role in Indian revolution. To miss this reality is to miss the most important characteristic of Indian constitution.

These democratic rights were won in the course of prolonged people's movement of which the communist were the most active segments.

India's socio economic structure

India's economy is built around a powerful public sector. This is a characteristic feature of the country's socio economic and political life. The main economic political and ideological battles in independent India have been fought around this question.

There took place sharp struggles between the forces of progress and reaction on public sector, nationalization, privy purses, building of heavy machinery and heavy industry. The dialects of struggle between the forces of progress and reaction has been distinguishing feature of post-independence India.

The forces belonging to extreme rightwing and extreme leftwing have consistently opposed these policies and were supported by world imperialism led by US. The elimination of feudalism and colonialism also had been main agenda of this struggle.

Threat of LPG: liberalization, privatization and globalization

The policies under the garb of globalization are in fact a cover of American strategy to bring the developing and other countries under its influence through various means. The US imperialism is using market mechanism to control the economies of other countries for its own purpose.

The struggle against LPG is part and parcel of these policies of world domination. They are at the same time the struggle to protect India's economy, particularly its public sector. It is around and based upon public sector. It is around and based upon public sector that further growth is possible. It does not mean at all the there should be no privatization or globalization or the entry of foreign private capital. They will definitely be needed in selective areas because every country can not produce everything. But it has to be done without compromising nation's basic policies of self-reliance end economic independence.

Nature of Indian bourgeoisie

Its nature is contradictory. It has grown out of India's freedom movement. Therefore, basically it is anti-imperialist, anti-colonial. Its policies and course of independent economic system have inherent anti-imperialist nature. It is still mainly based upon a powerful public sector, despite certain amount of disinvestment. A vast small and medium scale private industrial and economic sector has grown around and based upon it. Thus public /state sector continues to be the core of Indian economy.

STR nod changing composition of Indian society

The Indian society is undergoing rapid socio-economic and structural transformations which need to be analyzed properly. They have a direct bearing on strategy and tactics of struggle for transformation of the Indian society. These changes are part and parcel of world-wide changes.

Democratic revolution in India

Today there are far greater possibilities of involving the widest sections of classes and masses including working people and sections of capitalist and middle level classes in democratic transformations. A historic bloc of all these forces is possible. The institutions of transformation are open, legal and parliamentary and supported by mass people's actions they can become effective means of change. Media plays a crucial role.

Conclusion

I propose to return once again to what we, as concerned citizens could and should do to use media in furtherance of democratic value system. We have been hearing a lot about the decisive role played by internet and various social media sites during political upheavals in Egypt, Libya and even in India in Anna hazare's campaign against corruption. The self-laudary claims made by the new media instruments are no doubt exaggerated, but what prevents us from taking advantage of opportunity presented by these technological tools? I suggest all progressive organizations think tanks; even political parties should optimally use those becoming members and start posting material on these sites.

The simple point is that we have to adopt a two-prolonged strategy. One is continue to put pressure on elected governments for implementation of media policy that is in sync with the basic fabric of our society. The second is to keep exploring possibilities of people's initiatives in this direction.

Comment by Sarvesh Dutt Tripathi

No interlink between the beginning, middle and the end of the paper. The paper overall appears to be mere a suggestion to Indian people.

Media Convergence, ICT & Cultural Imperialism

Sushil Rai*

Abstract

In present Scenario, we are passing through the digital ag and media industries are grappling with new opportunities - and threats - afforded by what is called "convergence". Media people tend to get very excited about convergence, because it holds so many promises. Media convergence has transformed the communications We can view, hear, or read virtually anything, anywhere and anytime. As new services become widely available, they are changing the ways in which we live and work. Simultaneously we can realize that Western powers are extending their grip over the world not only politically and economically, but also culturally. This study will review what convergence and ICT means and how these are helping the current order and development of cultural imperialism? This study will find out the role and significance of Convergence & ICT. This paper will also explore the intensive relations between Convergence and cultural Imperialism at all possible angles and will provide vivid trends and impacts of Cultural imperialism thoroughly.

Keywords: Convergence, ICT, Global Culture, Imperialism, Multi-media, Mediamorphosis.

Assistant Professor
School of Mass Communication
IMS, Dehradun

Introduction

In present Scenario, we are passing through the digital age and media industries are grappling with new opportunities - and threats - afforded by what is called "convergence". Media people tend to get very excited about convergence, because it holds so many promises. The melding together of different media, incorporating new personalized services is both impressive and overwhelming. Media convergence has transformed the communications. And the adoption of high-performance computers, shift to digital platforms, and creation of high-speed computer networks and other media have brought us new ways of doing thing. Old barriers of time and space are practically eliminated. We can view, hear, or read virtually anything, anywhere and anytime. The old definitions that provided separation between Radio, TV, Cable, Newspapers, and Film have gone or are going forever. The 1990's brought ownership convergence, creating media conglomerates like Disney, Viacom, and Sony. From the consumer view, the Internet has recently changed our favorite delivery systems - Newspapers now provide video, TV offers interactive chat, and radio has web-cams.

With 3G telephony, mass media companies can include consumer technologies such as mobile phones and videogames. We have blurred the lines between info-tainment, promo-tainment, and edu-tainment, and now it's hard to separate intrapersonal, interpersonal, and mass communication. These changes represent a seismic shift in the way we view communication, and are typically referred to as Convergence media is implied.

The World Wide Web (WWW) gives users choice regarding external information. This reflects the traditional concept of Mass Communication. Although going to web sites is considered an active behavior, the consumer is still a receiver of information. Our respondents indicated that News and Information, Music, and Film content are especially popular. A second related technology is the mobile phone. This interpersonal communication technology empowers the user to be a sender/creator of thoughts, opinions, and ideas. With the option of either connecting to the WWW or acting as a stand-alone device for leisure gaming or content creation, the computer is a device that enables the user to create, send, and receive content. Finally, the multimedia computer is vital to convergence.

Media Convergence: Meaning & its importance

Convergence in general, it is a process of coming together or becoming more a like. But in specific way it has vast meaning in today's world. Convergence is more than technical term and process; it represents a reconfiguration of media power and a reshaping of media aesthetics and economics. The French cyberspace theorist Pierre Levy uses the term 'collective intelligence' to describe the large-scale information gathering and processing activities that have emerged in web communities. On the internet, he argues, people harness their individual expertise towards shared goals and objectives: 'No one knows everything, everyone knows something, all knowledge resides in humanity'.

The new knowledge culture has arisen as our ties to older forms of social community are breaking down, our rooting in physical geography is diminishing, our bonds to the extended and even the nuclear family are disintegrating and our allegiances to nation states are being redefined. However, new forms of community are emerging. These new communities are defined through voluntary, temporary and tactical affiliations, are reaffirmed through common intellectual enterprises and emotional investments and are held together through the mutual production and reciprocal exchange of knowledge.

Media convergence is the tendency for different technological systems to evolve toward performing similar tasks. Convergence can refer to previously separate technologies such as voice (and telephony features), data (and productivity applications), and video that now share resources and interact with each other synergistically. The rise of digital communication in the late 20th century has made it possible for media organizations or individuals to deliver text, audio, and video material over the same wired, wireless, or fiber-optic connections. At the same time, it inspired some media organizations to explore multimedia delivery of information. This digital convergence of news media, in particular, was called "Mediamorphosis" by researcher Roger Fiddler, in his 1997 book by that name. Today, we are surrounded by a multi-level convergent media world where all modes of communication and information are continually reforming to adapt to the enduring demands of technologies, "changing the way we create, consume, learn and interact with each other".

Convergence in this instance is defined as the interlinking of computing and other information technologies, media content, and communication networks that has arisen as the result of the evolution and popularization of the Internet as well as the activities, products and services that have emerged in the digital media space. Many experts view this as simply being the tip of the iceberg, as all facets of institutional activity and social life such as business, government, art, journalism, health, and education are increasingly being carried out in these digital media spaces across a growing network of information and communication technology devices.

Convergence generally means the intersection of old and new media. Jenkins states that convergence is, "the flow of content across multiple media platforms, the cooperation between multiple media industries, and the migratory behavior of media audiences."

Media convergence is not just a technological shift or a technological process; it also includes shifts within the industrial, cultural, and social paradigms that encourage the consumer to seek out new information. Convergence, simply put, is how individual consumers interact with others on a social level and use various media platforms to create new experiences, new forms of media and content that connect us socially, and not just to other consumers, but to the corporate producers of media in ways that have not been as readily accessible in the past. Therefore, Media convergence, in reality, is more than just a shift in technology. It alters relationships between industries, technologies, audiences, genres and markets. Media convergence changes the rationality media industries operate in, and the way that media consumers process news and entertainment. Media convergence is essentially a process and not an outcome, so no single black box controls the flow of media. With proliferation of different media channels and increasing portability of new telecommunications and computing technologies, we have entered into an era where media constantly surrounds us.

Information and Communication Technology

If we talk about communication system, undoubtedly convergence of the media has transformed the communications. As new services become widely available, they are changing the ways in which we live and work. And this change has been made due to development of Information and Communication Technology (ICT) which includes a range of technologies - used to support communication and information. ICT covers the areas of both networks and applications. Networks include fixed, wireless and satellite telecommunications networks, broadcasting networks. Although the area is much broader, well-known applications are the Internet, Geographic Information Systems, Database Management Systems, Multi-media tools, etc. ICT is quickly changing the world, creating a distance-less, borderless world of instantaneous communication. Increasingly, ICT is becoming less costly. Thus, ICT has much potential to create opportunities for growth and development in the rural areas of each state and society.

Relation between Media Convergence, ICT & Cultural Imperialism

Media convergence & ICT both has influenced our culture, behavior & ideology and simultaneously it has become a prominent tool to lead cultural imperialism. The Information Communication Technology especially Internet is allowing people to continue to participate in their "local" culture no matter where in the world they are. It is playing very important role and becoming very prominent tool for the preservation and celebration of culture and cultural imperialism too.

The cultural imperialism thesis has long been a central, as well as problematic, element of political economy approaches to global media. The Frankfurt School and the homogeneous school of thought identify the dominance model, which proposes that globalization leads to homogenization of culture through media and cultural imperialism. The cultural imperialism debate gained momentum after decolonization led to new states in Africa, Asia and the Pacific. Scholars replaced colonialism with a new form of capitalist subjugation of the Third World: neo-colonialism, which was more economic than political, more ideologically than militarily supported. Scholars argued that neo-colonialist powers turned to symbolic means of control, which was facilitated by the integration of global telecommunications systems and the proliferation of television. Armand Matterlart (1979), Herbert Schiller (1991) and Oliver Boyd Barrett (1977) have proposed cultural and media imperialist theories. The mass media, fitting in with the spread of global capitalism, push mainly American culture that promotes ideologies of consumption, instant gratification, and individualism. The cultural imperialism thesis argues that media globalization will lead to a homogenization of culture, identity and locale. Boyd-Barrett, one of the original proponents of media imperialism (1977), has revised his thesis to take into account different types of audiences, but argues that media imperialism remains a useful analytical concept.

Cultural imperialism

Imperialism is the domination of one country on the political, economic, or cultural life of another country. Imperialism is more often than not fueled by two major schools of thought known as nationalism and Social Darwinism. Nationalism is a feeling of pride and devotion to one's country. This can drive a person to think that their country is the most powerful, and in essence drives that person mad with power and a hunger to conquer, which not ironically is exactly what many countries did. Social Darwinism is the very idea that a more powerful country conquers the smaller countries. "Survival of the fittest," as the well renowned Charles Darwin used to say. Imperialism is also sometimes sparked by military motives, such as when USA set up a naval-marine base in the Philippines, and Economic Motives, which will be the main focus of the Imperialism of India by Britain. India's conquer by Britain is a perfect example of the pros and cons to an imperialistic world.

Regarding the question of globalizing culture and cultural diversity, the conflict perspective states that cultural globalization or cultural imperialism is a threat to indigenous cultures as these are progressively brought into contact with the global economy. Western powers extend their grip over the world not only politically and economically, but also culturally, by flooding other societies with their own cultural products (movies, television programs, and music), technology and values (individualism, consumption).

Cultural imperialism is the practice of imposing one's cultural products and values onto other societies, whether they want it or not, destroying native cultures in the process. The ultimate result is to create a culturally homogenous world of consumers for global capitalism. Cultural imperialism eliminates global diversity. Culture is the ideology of the capitalist world-system, or geoculture. Culture is not neutral but shaped by Western powers so as to create hegemony and maintain the unequal division of labor in the world-system. Cultural differences between countries are just devices to maintain the competitive nature of the system. That system needs consumers and therefore, the dominant values of the emerging global culture emphasize individualism and consumption. Such values contribute to maintaining the system.

The world-wide dominance and ubiquity of U.S. popular culture is viewed by many countries as cultural imperialism. Countries such as France and Canada believe that the books, films, and television programs that are created within their borders help define the very identity of their country. Those cultural products of today are being overwhelmed by the sheer volume of imports from the U.S.

The government of China is concerned with maintaining the current governmental structure, and the importation of Western culture brings with it ideas such as democracy, ideas the Chinese can do without. Singapore is struggling to preserve a national ideology and value system which the government believes is being threatened by unwanted outside influences.

Already, these countries are inundated with movies, books, and television programming from the U.S. As the popularity of the Internet grows, and as more multimedia content is being distributed via the Internet, countries are beginning to pass regulations and policies concerning Internet access and content available to their citizens.

The Threat of ICT as an Internet

If we talk about the threat of ICT as an Internet, we can understand easily, how Internet is becoming a prominent tool to generate and spread the dominant culture. It is estimated that 90% of the world-wide traffic on the Internet is in English. Combined with the fact that the Internet is based in the U.S., most Web sites are in the U.S. and are in English, most software used to navigate the Internet are in English, and search engines are mostly in English, have led some to denounce the Internet as the most recent and most sinister facet of American cultural imperialism to emerge.

It is believed by many that the Internet will be a driving force for the Anglicization of the world and that English, currently the unofficial language of world commerce, will become that of world culture. This has led, for example, to attempts by the European Parliament to legislate culture. The Parliament has asked for controls on the Internet including extending quotas and controls on content for multimedia services transmitted on the Internet.

In France, cultural identity is tied up with the French language. The nation's cultural production defines its very identity - the Frenchness that is France. A major objection to U.S. products is that they are in English. Inundated with U.S. popular culture, the French government fears that people will feel like tourists in their own country.

There is a basic difference in perception between Americans and the French towards cultural production. Americans tend to view television programs, films, and books as commercial products created by the private sector. The French see culture as defining them as a nation, and accept the government's role to restrict the importation of cultural goods. The French arguments to restrict the onslaught of American goods go beyond mere marketplace competition; they truly believe their cultural identity is at stake. The French government is concerned that the Internet will be another tool for U.S. cultural imperialism. The French people are already wired for computers, having used Minitels for many years. The problem with the Minitel system is that it is text-based and relatively slow. The growing popularity of PCs and the Internet has alarmed the government, which has renewed its call for quotas on foreign cultural content delivered via the World Wide Web.

It is possible that new information communication technologies such as the Internet and satellite broadcasting will make culture quotas obsolete. There is little that can be done to control the content of information disseminated by way of mediums which do not respect geographical boundaries except to enforce a total ban on the receiving systems such as satellite dishes. Nations such as France or Canada worried about the threat posed by the Internet to dilute or eliminate cultural to focus on production and dissemination of their own cultural products online.

Therefore, other countries like Singapore, Hong Kong, Russia, Japan, China India etc. all are struggling to preserve a national ideology and value system which is being threatened by unwanted outside cultural influences by new setup of information communication technology.

In the context of maintaining cultural diversity and different morals and lifestyles, it is hard to fault the Singapore government in its attempt to regulate the Internet. It is not always best that American culture, our attitudes and our capitalism, be exported to every region of the world.

In China, Chinese leaders also perceive the Internet as threatening their governmental system of autocratic rule. It is believed that the Internet will allow the dissemination of ideas, democracy among them, which will lead to the downfall of the communist government.In 1995, China began a program to increase content control over the Internet. First, it forced the U.S. to accept Chinese political censorship practices in return for commercial access to the country's vast music market. Second, its Ministry of Posts and Telecommunications directed all Internet providers to restrict access to undesirable political discussions. As a result, the China Internet Corporation, a subsidiary of the official Chinese news agency Xinhua, declared that it would eliminate newsgroups, ftp sites, and the like that are not related to business.

On February 4, 1996, the Chinese government announced that it intended to increase control over the Internet. Computer networks would be forced to use approved links as well as prohibited from moving any information deemed a hindrance to public order. The rules are meant to strengthen the hold of the Ministry of Posts and Telecommunications, who will manage all networks over the Internet by forcing all networks to liquidate and reregister.

Therefore, these above mentioned instances are clearly indicating about the impact of cultural imperialism and its threats among the nations through out world. really the ICT has changed the whole method of communication and momentum of media which has influenced the societies and peoples on global level.

Simultaneously it has also created a strong voice for dominant cultures, western culture especially US Culture. John states, 'American culture is global culture.' That does mean that it is perfect or even necessarily good but that is the closest thing that exist to universalism. Since the majority of internet culture is dominantly American flavored. Thus western cultures and values threatens to overshadow all other cultures around the world and in this reference ICT and Media convergence both are playing very vital roles.

Conclusion:

Undoubtedly the rise of ICT & digital media both have accelerated the pace of communication development and they are becoming more powerful with each new application. These technologies have given us ability to cross a border with touch of a button. As a medium really it is powerful due to the numerous method of contact; one to one, one to many and many to many. Its speed is almost instantaneous and its popularity is increasing almost exponentially. The evolution of ICT has blurred the national boundaries and pushed for universal culture. ICT has given us the era of globalization in which we are living, working and moving without having long distances. With increasing mobility, we are being influenced by dominant culture which is actively shaping and taking part in another country's cultural life. Therefore, not only a single territory, society or a state is feeling the strength of cultural imperialism but each corner of the world are gradually coming under the shadow of global culture. And if we think how the flow of news and culture is encompassing the globe and drawing us into a single Marshal Mcluhan's 'global village' in which global culture is growing, we will find out the reason easily that it is happening just because of improved ICT and convergence of distinct media technology.

Bibliography:

1. Chada, K. and Kavoori, A. (2000). Media Imperialism Revisited:

Some Findings From the Asian Case. Media, Culture and Society, 22(4), 415-32.

2. Madhavan, Shobhana. (2011). Cross-Cultural Management: Concept and cases, New Delhi: Oxford University Press
3. Castells, M. (2009). Communication Power. New York: Oxford University Press.
4. Gillespie, M. (1995). Television, Ethnicity and Cultural Change. London: Rutledge.
5. Golding, P. and Harris, P. (Eds.). (1997). Beyond Cultural Imperialism: Globalization, Communication and the New International Order. London: Sage.
6. Griffin, M. (2002). From Cultural Imperialism to transnational commercialization: Shifting paradigms in international media studies. Global Media Journal, 1(1).
7. Lievrouw, L. A. and Livingstone, S. M. (2006). (Ed.) Handbook of New Media: Social Shaping and Social Consequences of ICTs. London: Sage.
8. Rantanen, T. (2005).The Media and Globalization. London: Sage.
9. Wahl-Jorgensen, K. & Hanitzsch, T (Eds.). (2008). Convergence and Cross-Platform Content Production. London: Routledge.
10. D.B. Abernethy, The Dynamics of Global Dominance: European Overseas Empires, 1415 1980 (Yale University Press; New Have & London, 2000)
11. R. Falk, A Worldwide Religious Resurgence in an Era of Globalisation, in, F. Petito & P. Hatzopoulos (Edtd.), Religion in International Relations: the Return from Exile (Palgrave Macmillan; New York, 2003)
12. J.M. Mackenzie, Introduction, in, J.M. Mackenzie (Edtd.), Imperialism and Popular Culture (Manchester University Press; Manchester, 1994)

13. J. Sinclair, E. Jacka & S. Cunningham, Peripheral Vision, in, F.J. Lechner & J. Boli (Edtd.), The Globalisation Reader, Second Edition (Blackwell; Oxford, 2004)
14. http://www.gov.sg/sba/netreg/annexa.htm
15. Singapore Broadcasting Authority Internet Content Guidelines, Annex C
16. Singapore Broadcasting Authority, News Release, July 11, 1996
17. Tony Walker, Beijing Tightens Rules on Access to Internet, Financial Times, Feb. 5, 1996
18. Tony Walker, Beijing Tightens Rules on Access to Internet, Financial Times, Feb. 5, 1996
19. A Report for Howard Besser's Class on Impact of New Information Resources: Multimedia and Networks Stephen Morris - December 5, 1996
20. http://www.item.ntnu.no/fag/ttm4/YZYauGlobalization ICTSAfrica.pdf
21. http://www.ideaconnection.com/solutions/554-Cultural-imperialism.html

Comment by Sarvesh Dutt Tripathi

In my opinion well written but least reference is given in the text. Everything appears to be the opinion of the writer himself.

ICT- Revolutionizes E-commerce and E-Business

Gaurav Yadav*

Abstract

In the emerging global economy, E-commerce and E-Business have increasingly become a necessary component of business strategy and a strong catalyst for economic development. The integration of information and communications technology (ICT) in business has revolutionized relationships within organizations and those between and among organizations and individuals. Specifically, the use of ICT in business has enhanced productivity, encouraged greater customer participation, and enabled mass customization, besides reducing costs.

With developments in the Internet and Web-based technologies, distinctions between traditional markets and the global electronic marketplace-such as business capital size are gradually being narrowed down. E-Business is a new business paradigm, a new concept floating around for some years now. It helps connect stakeholders electronically at any time and anywhere around the world. It is a business in cyberspace providing equal opportunity to everybody who has access to Internet Technology. E-Business (electronic business),is the conduct of business on the Internet, not only buying and selling but also servicing customers and collaborating with business partners. It is

* *Lecturer, Lingaya's Lalita Devi Institute of Management & Scinces*

one of the catalysts for globalised economic activities which have brought enormous wealth to some countries in the developed world. Some developing countries, for example, India is reaping benefit out of the globalization. Rapid technological change is having a profound influence on how we organize and conduct businesses. More significantly, the Internet makes it possible to transform electronic trading from an expensive and specialized process into a cheap and convenient method for all. This paper will depict the investment done by the organization in E-commerce especially in B2B and B2C model. The paper will also highlight the revenues earned by the countries and organizations through E-commerce specially in context with Amazon.com. The secondary data will be used for the research. The paper will elaborate the Impact of recession on E-commerce Investment and revenue generation. The finding and suggestions expected to come up after the research will provide input for further improvements and future Prospects of E-Business.

Introduction:

Until the last few centuries, there were two main Revolutions - the Industrial Revolution and the Electronic Revolution. The Industrial revolution transformed our society from agricultural based to industrial based and the electronic revolution transferred our society from mechanical to electronic based. This 21st Century is the beginning of new revolution, i.e. network revolution. It interconnects the different parts of the world together and the concept of globalisation comes into existence. The internet is the engine of this revolution and E-commerce is the fuel. The idea of conducting business transaction via electronic media is an integral part of many businesses for several decades. But due to the advancement of internet technologies and advanced cryptographic techniques, E-commerce comes into the existence.

Evolution of Commerce: Commerce has evolved over the centuries. Prior to the evolution of money, it was a simple barter process; the evolution of money brought with it the concept of "market place". In market place, commerce is function of 4p's - Product, Price, Place and Promotion. It was realised that with the slightest modification of 2Ps i.e. Price and Place, can bring the convenience to the customer of getting product at their home. With this concept of street vendor was born, afterwards the concept of mail-order cataloguing and tele-shopping came into existence with development of media vehicle

Barter Process

↓

Monetary Transactions

↓

Street Vendors

↓

Mail Order Cataloguing

↓

Tele Shopping

↓

Electronic Commerce

The latest generation of commerce is one that can be done over internet. Internet provides a virtual platform to buyers and sellers to sell and buy the goods and services. The commerce over internet is known as "Electronic commerce" or "E-commerce".E-commerce has emerged as boundary less trade medium in the era of globalisation.

Global recession: A global recession is a period of global economic slowdown. The International Monetary Fund (IMF) takes many factors into account when defining a global recession, it states that global economic growth of 3% or less is "equivalent to a global recession".

Recession: Period of general economic decline, defined usually as a contraction in the GDP for six months (two consecutive quarters) or longer.

Electronic Business: It is commonly referred as "E-Business", it may be defined as the utilization of information and communication technologies (ICT) in support of all the activities of business.

Electronic Commerce: Electronic commerce or E-commerce (E com) is a subset of E-Business. E-commerce is the purchasing, selling, and exchanging of goods and services over computer networks (such as the Internet) through which transactions or terms of sale are performed electronically.

Types of Ecommerce: Ecommerce can be broken into four main categories:

- **B2B (Business-to-Business):** Companies doing business with each other such as manufacturers selling to distributors and wholesalers selling to retailers. Pricing is based on quantity of order and is often negotiable. Like alibaba.com is B2B website.
- **B2C (Business-to-Consumer):** Businesses selling to the general public typically through catalogs utilizing shopping cart software. Google is the good example of B2C website.
- **C2B (Consumer-to-Business):** A consumer posts his project with a set budget online and within hours companies review the consumer's requirements and bid on the project. The consumer reviews the bids and selects the company that will complete the project. Ebay.com is C2B website.
- **C2C (Consumer-to-Consumer):** where individuals can buy and sell thanks to online payment systems like Paypal where people can send and receive money online with ease.

New technological innovation: E-Business

Year 1830-1900 was a time of rapid economic growth and technological innovation which has been well documented and analyzed. Business historians Chandler (1977) and Porter and Livesay (1971) discuss changing patterns of production and distribution over this period.

In 1830, almost all goods were generic. Production processes used relatively simple technology and were low volume, with nearly all products distributed within a small locality. The historical trend identified is the increasingly concentrated nature of the market, and the reduced costs of exchange. Changes in technology and market conditions created an economic situation that favored manufacturer-controlled distribution systems. However, that new technology (E-Business) is an important contributing factor to the changing organizational structure of firms. The four ways in which technological innovations can have impact: by necessitating new organizational structures to handle complexities, by encouraging administrative or other process changes that reduce costs or improve efficiency, by facilitating the development of new distribution channels, and by changing the power relations amongst organizations.

E-Business Worldwide:

With over 1.2 billion Internet users worldwide in 2007, E-commerce has seen unprecedented growth over the last decade. Most retailers have taken advantage of this lucrative arena and have created a presence on the Internet, targeting the immense buying power of worldwide online shoppers. In 2009, online spending by consumers online purchases will rise by a substantial 13.3% to £20.9 billion although the internet is undoubtedly starting to slow and become a much more competitive environment, online retail is still set to reach £31.2 billion by 2013, accounting for 10.0% of total retail spending. In 2009, total retail growth will contract by 0.6% as consumer spending is ravaged by the effects of the recession.

However, the online market will expand by a substantial 13.3% over the course of the year, driven by the continued increases in the number of internet shoppers and higher expenditure per head. This follows on from the trend of 2008 when there was a 1.0% increase in internet users-to 34.4m-and an 18.1% increase in online shoppers-to 26.7m-with each of these individuals spending an average of 5.8% more in comparison to 2007. Although online growth in 2008 represented a substantial out performance of wider retail, it was also the smallest rise in the channel's sales since the dotcom bubble burst in 2002. There are a growing number of signs that the internet is beginning to mature and enter a new, more subdued phase of growth, Growth in the number of online shoppers in 2008 was strong, but considerably less than the growth seen in 2007. It is predicted that these growth rates will continue to fall over the next five years, as penetration of the population begins to level out.

Korea's total E-commerce transaction for year 2006-2007 is

Transaction Category	2006 (US $ thousand)		2007 (US $ thousand)		COMPARISION 2006 vs 2007 (US $ thousand)	
		RATE		RATE		
E-commerce						
Total	413,584	100%	516,514	100%	102.930	24.9%
B2B	366,191	88.3%	464,456	89.9%	98,264	26.8%
B2C	9,132	2.2%	10,226	2.0%	1,094	2%
C2C	3,826	0.9%	5,032	1.0%	1,206	31.5%

The **world wide E-commerce** transactions are

YEAR	US$ Billion	YEAR	US$ Billion
2007	240	2006	190
2005	150	2004	130
2003	100	2002	80
2001	70	2000	50
1999	25	1998	10

The share of B2B in total global E-commerce was 79.2% during 2000 and rose to 87% during 2004. According to the regions B2B E-commerce in $ billions during 2000-04 were as under

Year/Region	2000	2001	2002	2003	2004	As % of world wide B2B commerce 2004
North America	159.2	316.8	563.9	964.3	1600.8	57.7
Asia/ Pacific	36.2	68.6	121.2	199.3	300.6	10.8
Europe	26.2	52.4	132.7	334.1	797.3	28.7
Latin America	2.9	7.9	17.4	33.6	58.4	2.1
Africa/ Middle East	1.7	3.2	5.9	10.6	17.7	0.6
Total	226.2	448.9	841.1	1541.9	2774.8	100

The worldwide sales for B2B category is

YEAR	B2B Sales (including EDI) US$ Billion
2007	6800
2006	5300
2005	4100
2004	2800
2003	1600
2002	900
2001	730
2000	600
1999	550
1998	520

The world wise E-commerce revenue in percentage in year 2000 and 2004 was

Region	Year 2000	Year 2004
Asia	5%	10%
Western Europe	46%	83%
Rest of the world	7%	7%

E-Business in India

The low cost of the PC and the growing use of the Internet has shown the tremendous growth of Ecommerce in India, in the recent years. According to the Indian Ecommerce Report released by Internet and Mobile Association of India (IAMAI) and IMRB International, "The total online transactions in India was Rs. 7080 crores (approx $1.75 billion) in the year 2006-2007 and grow by 30% to touch 9210 crores (approx $2.15 billion) by the year 2007-2008. Although, as compared to the western countries, India is still in is its initial stage of development. Although business-to-business transactions play an important part in E-commerce market, a share of E-commerce revenues in developed countries is generated from business to consumer transactions. Railway and Airlines have played a vital role in E-commerce transactions in India. Travel portals are exploding in India. Recently MakeMyTrip.com has shown Rs 1000 crores of turnover. Travel alone constituted 50% of Rs 4800 crore online market in 2007-08. In India, online services like ticketing, banking, tax payment, bill payment, hotel room booking, entertainment, online games, matrimonial sites, job sites, etc. are showing signs of development in business-to-customer transactions. There has been tremendous boost in the online E-Business with the stock exchange coming online. Online valentine gifts and Diwali gifts are also becoming popular along with the birthday cakes. No doubt, the total value of the B2B transactions is much larger than that of the B2C transactions, because typically B2B transactions are of much greater value than B2C transactions. It seems that the B2C market in India will take time to grow as compared to the B2B market.

E-Business in the Era of Recession

The economic downturn is leading to the internet playing an increasingly bigger role. The net effect of the recession is likely to make the web a bigger part of retailing because retail chains and consumer goods manufacturers have seen during the recession how consumers use the web to research, even if they buy offline. Actual purchase is not the only aspect of online shopping for customers.

According to the report by Forrester Research and others on E-commerce indicates that E-commerce is one of the very few markets with growth expectations in 2009 and beyond. According to the report E-commerce revenue will grow from $204B to $335B by 2012. It has been believed that online sales will continue to grow through the recession due to accelerating shifts in consumer buyer patterns.

Drop in real U.S. GDP of 1.5% to 1.9% occurs for three to four quarters, it is believed that online retail E-commerce would still increase by 18%. In US the E-commerce rose 14.3% in 2008, but 26.5% overseas. That adds up to 21.5% combined, and even if economic growth slows globally

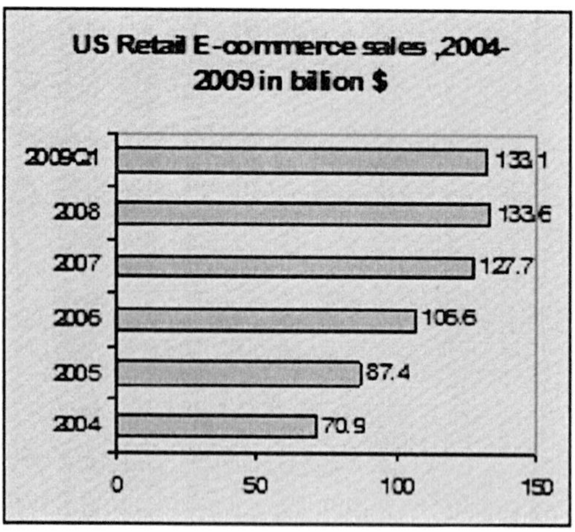

Performance of various B2B and B2C Companies in the Era of Recession

1. Amazon

Company seeks to offer the Earth's Biggest Selection and to be the Earth's most customer- centric company, where customers can find and discover anything they may want to buy online.

Amazon.com, Inc. operates as an online retailer in North America and internationally. It operates various retail Web sites, including amazon.com, amazon.co.uk, amazon.de, amazon.fr, amazon.co.jp, amazon.ca, and amazon.cn. The company serves its consumer customers through its retail Websites and focuses on selection, price, and convenience. It also offers programs that enable seller customers to sell their products on its Websites and their own branded Websites. In addition, the company serves developer customers through Amazon Web Services, which provides access to technology infrastructure that developers can use to enable virtually any type of business. Further, it offers co-branded credit card programs, fulfillment, and other marketing and promotional services, such as online advertising. Amazon.com, Inc. was founded in 1994 and is headquartered in Seattle, Washington.

If Amazon's 66 million active customers all lived in the same country, it would be the world's 19th most populous country, larger than every European country except Germany. And if every US household spent $170 at Amazon.com this year, the total amount they'd spend would still be less than Amazon's 2008 revenues of over $19B. Amazon has used the internet to create a truly global business platform, one which is poised for incredible growth in the coming decade. Sales have surged year over year at the world's largest E-commerce company, with revenues growing 29.1% from 2007 to 2008 due to a combination of low prices, shipping promotions, and rollouts of new product categories.

While most people naturally think of Amazon as the internet superstore that sells products in over forty categories, from books to electronics to groceries to jewellery to auto parts, the company has gradually expanded beyond that simple E-Business platform; today Amazon is simultaneously an E-commerce and internet technology platform, a fulfillment and logistics platform, a search technology, an internet advertising platform, and even an internet start up incubator of sorts.

Recent stock performance

Amazon Historical Performance

Current Price (7/2/2009): 79.32

(Figures in U.S. Dollars)

Category Expansion

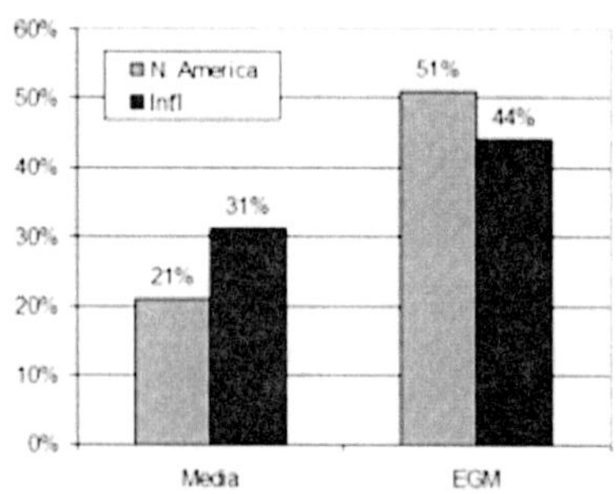

Although 64% of Amazon's worldwide revenue still comes from media categories (books, music, video), Amazon's product footprint in the US has expanded into over 40 categories. New product categories represent significant growth opportunities for the company, given the lower online penetration rates in many of these categories. Revenue and income growth rates for these categories have regularly outpaced the growth in media categories both in the US and abroad. Q3 2007 saw the launch of Apparel & Shoes, Home & Kitchen, and Baby stores for several of Amazon's international presences, and the highly successful Fulfilment by Amazon was expanded to the UK, Germany and Japan as well.

International Expansion

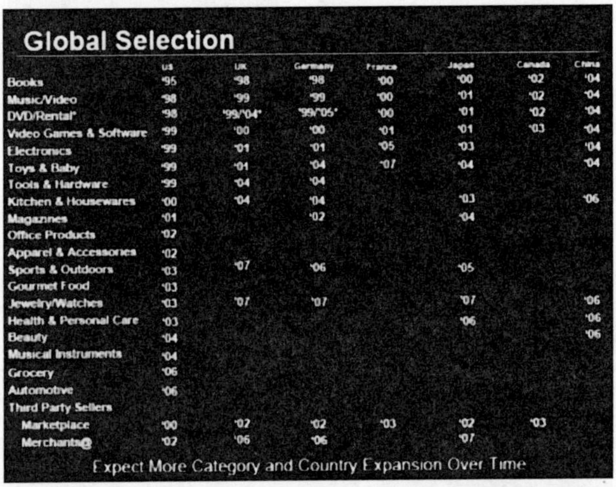

Global Selection

	US	UK	Germany	France	Japan	Canada	China
Books	'95	'98	'98	'00	'00	'02	'04
Music/Video	'98	'99	'99	'00	'01	'02	'04
DVD/Rental*	'98	'99/'04*	'99/'05*	'00	'01	'02	'04
Video Games & Software	'99	'00	'00	'01	'01	'03	'04
Electronics	'99	'01	'01	'05	'03		'04
Toys & Baby	'99	'01	'04	'07	'04		'04
Tools & Hardware	'99	'04	'04				
Kitchen & Housewares	'00	'04	'04		'03		'06
Magazines	'01		'02		'04		
Office Products	'02						
Apparel & Accessories	'02						
Sports & Outdoors	'03	'07	'06		'05		
Gourmet Food	'03						
Jewelry/Watches	'03	'07	'07		'07		'06
Health & Personal Care	'03				'06		'06
Beauty	'04						'06
Musical Instruments	'04						
Grocery	'06						
Automotive	'06						
Third Party Sellers							
Marketplace	'00	'02	'02	'03	'02	'03	
Merchants@	'02	'06	'06		'07		

Expect More Category and Country Expansion Over Time

International businesses have represented a significant area of growth for Amazon. Although Amazon ships to almost any country in the world, it has selectively chosen to establish country-specific websites and fulfilment networks. Beginning with its expansion into the UK and Germany in 1998, and subsequently to France (2000), Japan (2000), Canada (2002), and expansion into China, Amazon has expanded its geographic footprint into the world's major E-commerce markets. International growth rates have consistently beaten that of North America, with growth rates in revenue.

Business and Financials

	2006	2007	2008
Net Sales ($millions)	10,711	14,835	19,166
Net Income ($millions)	190	476	645
Operating expenses($millions)	1,966	2,513	3,153
Cash ($millions)	1,022	2,539	2,769
Current Ratio	N/A	1.39	1.30

Earnings Highlights (Q1 '09):

Amazon.com Inc. released first quarter earnings. Earnings climbed 24 percent to $177 million, or 41 cents per share, compared with $143 million, or 34 cents per share, in the year-ago quarter, to beat the 31 cents per share .

The revenue rose 18 percent to $4.89 billion, slightly higher than analysts' expectations of $4.76 billion. In the first quarter, sales of items such as books, CDs and DVDs rose 7 percent to $2.72 billion, while sales of electronics and other general merchandise rose nearly 39 percent to $2.05 billion.

Revenue/GPM: Amazon.com spent $3.74 billion to make $4.89 billion in revenue. This Gross Profit Margin totaled 23.5 %.

Comparison of Growth in Sales between Fiscal Years (2005-2008)

Years	FY08-FY07	FY07-FY06	FY06-FY05
North America (%)	26	38	25
International (%)	33	39	28

This is due in part to the relative maturity of the US market, as well as to the strategy Amazon has employed in rolling out new product categories and features to its international properties. Amazon has typically introduced most of its new stores and features in the US market first, eventually replicating the most successful ventures in international markets. Amazon's international businesses have thus been able to benefit from experience gained through US experiments to grow at an accelerated pace.

Revenue by Geography (USD)

Period Ending	31-Dec 2004	31-Dec 2005	31-Dec 2006	31-Dec 2007	31-Dec 2008
Revenue - North America	3.85B	4.71B	5.87B	8.10B	10.2B
Revenue - International	3.07B	3.78B	4.84B	6.74B	8.94B
Total Revenue	6.92B	8.49B	10.7B	14.8B	19.2B

Revenue by Segment (USD)

Period Ending	31-Dec 2004	31-Dec 2005	31-Dec 2006	31-Dec 2007	31-Dec 2008
Revenue - Media	5.10B	5.93B	7.07B	9.24B	11.1B
Revenue - Electronics & Other General Merchandise	1.69B	2.33B	3.36B	5.21B	7.54B
Total Revenue	6.92B	8.49B	10.7B	14.8B	19.2B

2. Google

Google Inc. is an American public Corporation, earning revenue from advertising related to its Internet search, email, online mapping, offline productivity, social networking and video sharing services as well as selling advertising-free versions of the same technologies. The Google headquarters, the googleplex, is located in Mounatain view, California. As of March 31, 2009, the company has 20,164 full-time employees. Google was founded by Larry Page and Sergey Brin while they were students at Stanford University and the company was first incorporated as a privately held company on September 4, 1998. The initial public offering took place on August 19, 2004, raising US$ 1.67 billion, implying a value for the entire corporation of US$23 billion. Google has continued its growth through a series of new product developments, acquisition, partnership, environmentalism; philanthropy and positive employee relation have been important tenets during the growth of Google. Google's mission is "to organize the world's information and make it universally accessible and useful".

The Investment made by the Google during the year 2006, 2007, 2008 and 2009Q1 is as follows

COST	2006	2007	2008	2009Q1
Costof revenues	4,225,027	6,649,085	8,621,506	2,101,504
Traffic Acquisition Cost	3,308,777	4,933,878	5,938,951	1,435,960

Other Cost of Revenues	916,250	1,715,207	2,682,555	665,544
Research & Development	1,228,589	2,119,985	2,793,192	641,643
Sales & Marketing	849,518	1,461,266	1,946,244	433,941
General & Administrative	751,787	1,279,250	1,802,639	448,311
Total Costs & Expenses	7,054,921	11,509,586	15,163,581	3,625,399

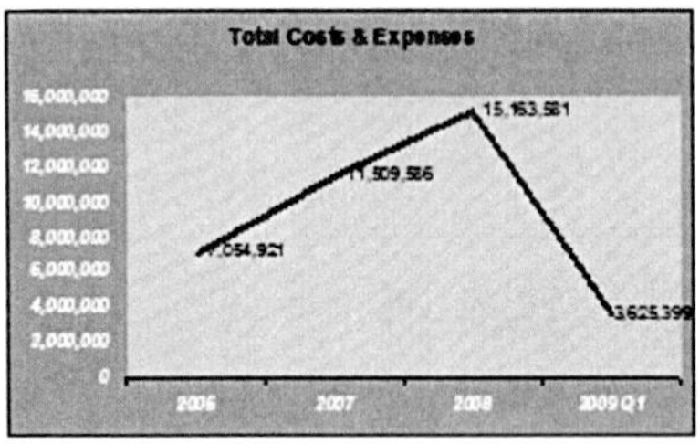

Even during the period of recession Google has invested more than the prior years.

Revenues earned by Google:

Revenues	2006	2007	2008	2009 Q1
Revenues	10,604,917	16,593,986	21,795,550	5,508,990
Google web sites	6,332,797	10,624,705	14,413,826	3,692,823
Google Network web sites	4,159,831	5,787,938	6,714,688	1,638,042
Total Advertising Revenues	10,492,628	16,412,643	21,128,514	5,330,865
Licensing & other revenues	112,289	181,343	667,036	178,125

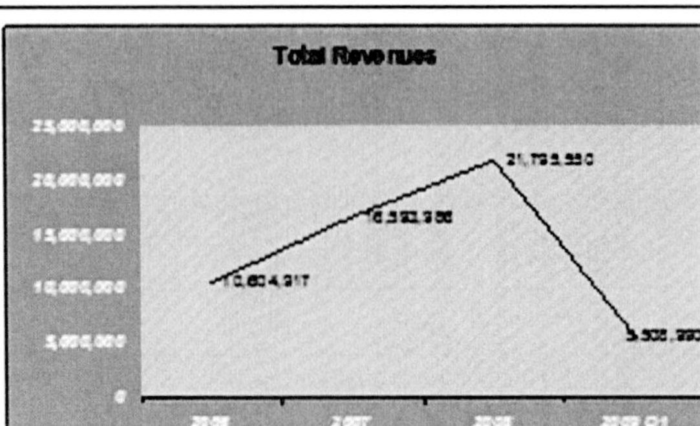

Google has earned good revenues during the period of recession, as the chart indicates the revenue is increasing year by year; there is les effect of recession on B2C companies.

3. Alibaba.com

Alibaba Group is a Hangzhou-based family of Internet-based businesses that include Business-to-business trade, online retail, a payment platform, and business management software and regionalized classified listings. It was founded in 1999 by Ma Yun (Jack Ma), and operates five E-commerce sub-companies which operate different aspects of trading. In 2008, alibaba.com attracted at least 23 million visitors of which 65 percent were from China. Japan's Softbank was one of the earliest investors in Alibaba. Its founder, Masayoshi Son, invested $18 million in the company in 2000 and also participated in subsequent rounds of financing.

As of January 2007, the Alibaba Group is made up of 5 sub-companies:

- **Alibaba.com:** English language global trade website serving small and medium-sized enterprises
- **Taobao.com:** Online auctions web site for customers
- **Alipay:** Online payments web site, processing mainly payments within China
- **Alisoft:** Provider of web services to the Chinese Small and Medium-sized Enterprise marketplace
- **Alimama:** Online advertising exchange, which allows web publishers and advertisers to trade online advertising inventory.

The Revenues earned and the investment made by the Alibaba during the year 2006, 2007, 2008 and 2009Q1 is as follows (in RMB'000)

COST	2006	2007	2008 Q1	2008 Q4	2009Q1
Cost of Revenue	237,625	280113	78,926	118,252	108,824
Sales and Marketing Expanses	610,198	736,813	201,743	371,286	288,963
Product and development expenses	105,486	131,495	36,592	62,828	60,539
General and Administrative expenses	159,969	229,868	72,210	93,113	83,885
Business Taxes and Surcharge	69,394	110,545	-	-	-
Bandwidth and depreciation expenses	30,983	38,771	-	-	-
Staff cost and other expenses	237,625	280,113	-	-	-

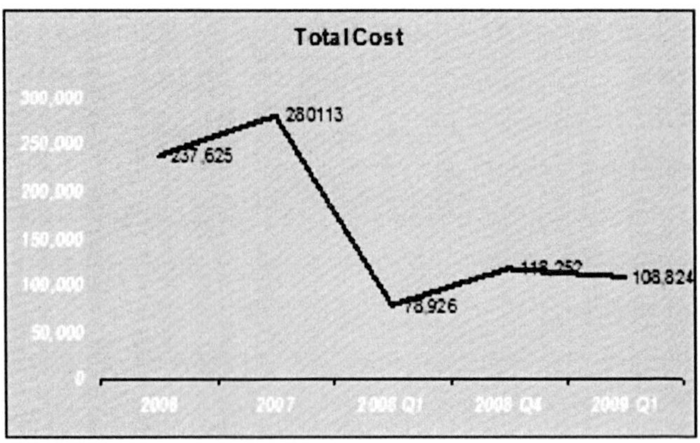

Revenues	2006	2007	2008 Q1	2008 Q4	2009 Q1
International market place					
Gold Supplier members	967,858	1,503,331	447,630	475,438	492,683
International Trust pass members	24,011	32,825	8,994	12,083	12,876
Other Revenues	-	11,539	7,540	1,583	-
Sub-total	991,869	1,547,695	46,164	489,104	505,559

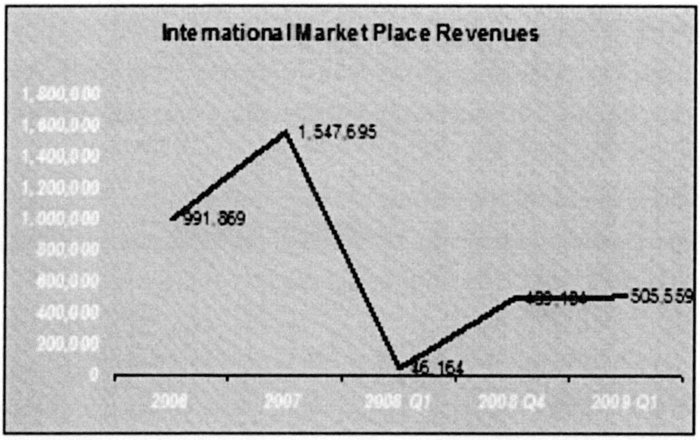

Revenues	2006	2007	2008 Q1	2008 Q4	2009 Q1
China market place					
China Trust pass members	369,653	594,098	206,127	294,070	288,468
Other Revenues	2,340	20,964	9,790	22,690	12,606
Sub-total	371,993	615,062	215,917	316,760	301,074

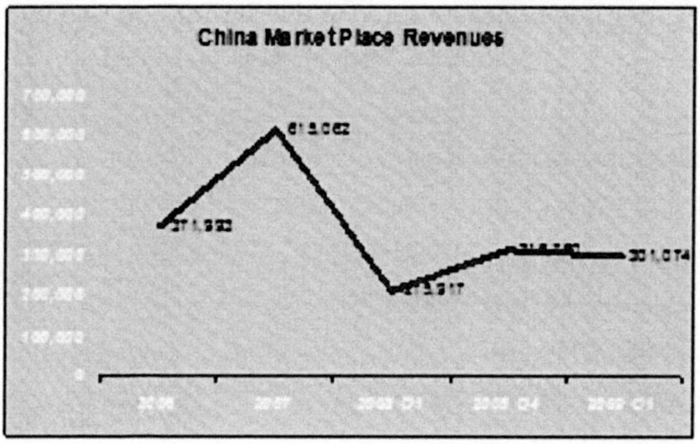

Revenues	2006	2007	2008 Q1	2008 Q4	2009 Q1
Revenues	1,363,862	2,162,757	78,926	118,252	108,824
International market place	991,869	1,547,695	464,164	489,104	505,559
China Market place	371,993	615,062	215,917	316,760	301,074

Key Highlights

- By 2012 it is expected that more than 1 trillion will be spent online by B2C Consumers.B2B spending will exceed this considerably.
- E-payment solutions are an important part of E-commerce transactions; however security issues continue to tarnish the industry.
- BuddeComm estimates revenue from mobile content and services (excluding SMS), accounts for around 7-10% of total mobile revenues worldwide. SMS remains popular and accounts for a further 10% of total mobile data revenues.
- Online advertising growth is set to continue for the next few years, but will slow slightly in the wake of the US financial crisis. It is expected that online advertising will eventually account for around 20% of all advertising spend in some markets.
- Search services are central to almost everything that users do online, and this places leading search companies such as Google and Yahoo at an advantage. In the emerging Chinese market, Baidu and Alibaba also have a good foothold.
- Google is still the most popular website property worldwide; however individual countries and regions show unique differences with many local sites remaining popular. Other web properties proving popular across multiple markets include Yahoo, Microsoft and Wikipedia sites, Apple Inc, eBay and Amazon.

Conclusion:

Preferences of online purchasing over stores

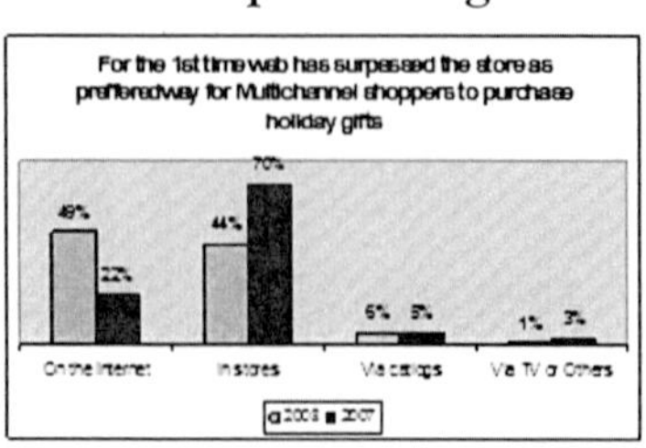

In 2008 the web has surpassed the stores for multichannel shoppers to purchase holiday gifts. In 2008 around 49% people purchased the products through web, while in 2007 this figure was 22% only. This shows that in recession has positive impact on E-commerce.

The future of E-commerce is going to depend upon a positive confluence of technology, regulation, laws. Culture, social issues, economics, vendors, competitors and all consumers. From the estimated future sales figures, that appears to be happening. Overall, E-commerce is and will be important for countries and firms that already possess the environment and the capabilities and capacity to utilize the Internet for sales purposes. While E-commerce may offer little initially to bring them to the industrial nation status, there will be dramatic increases in the well being of many third world countries. Economics, politics and competitive forces will also help bring them into the 21st Century of electronics, driven by the Internet that has no boundaries and is owned by no nation. A restructuring of worldwide channels of distribution will occur with concomitant new sales, sometimes to the detriment of existing industrialized nations, with a major contribution to the economic development of both industrialized and developing nations.

Even in this period of recession the E-commerce especially E-tailing, B2C companies have shown the growth towards positive side. When companies are cutting down their budgets, these companies are investing in E-Business during recession and reaping the profits because E-Business is a global business and the impact of recession is not same every where.

References

Books

- E-commerce-Business, technology, society 2008 by Kenneth .C.Laudon and Carlo Guercio Traver

Websites

www.emarketer.com/Reports/All/Emarketer_2000577.aspx

www.seekingalpha.com

www.shipwire.com/help/c/recession_proof_ecommerce_business/

www.en.wikipedia.org/wiki/Alibaba_Group

www.investor.google.com/earnings.html

www.google.com/finance?q=GOOG

www.investor.google.com/releases.html

www.blogs.zdnet.com/BTL/?p=8033

www.mattdecuir.com/Google/financials.aspx

www.img.alibaba.com/ir/download/200905/E_1Q09_Earnings Release.pdf

www.img.alibaba.com/ir/download/200803/Alibaba%20Earning%20Release_Eng.pdf

www.google.com

www.thehindubusinessline.com

www.harvardbusiness.org

www.protiviti.com/economiccrisis

http://www.wikinvest.com/stock/Amazon.com_(AMZN)?ref=topnav

http://jobsearchtech.about.com/od/companyprofiles/a/Amazon.htm

http://www.seattlepi.com/business/158315_amazon28.html

http://www.corporateinformation.com

http://www.crunchbase.com/company/amazon

http://www.chillibreeze.com/articles_various/Ecommerce.asp

http://wrightreports.ecnext.com/coms2/reportdesc_COMPANY_023135106

http://www.epaynews.com/item.php?news_id=6548

Amazon 1Q profit, revenue jump on strong sales

Comment by Sarvesh Dutt Tripathi

Good effort of compilation of data. The writer has confessed in the abstract that only secondary data will be used but at least he could have given the source of secondary data with every graphics. Anyway the paper is informative but it would have been better if in a small segment the original research would have been conducted in Delhi itself to substantiate all these secondary data.